GW00835952

RETICULATED
PYTHONS

Picture credits: Front cover - Natasha James and edited by Craig Frank,
page 1 - Natasha James, page 3 - Joanna Aldwinckle, page 4 - Tyree Jimerson

RETICULATED
PYTHONS

A COMPLETE GUIDE TO CARE AND HUSBANDRY

SID JAMES

CONTENTS

Introduction

The aim of this book is twofold. The first is to bring together an illustrated set of topics on reticulated pythons that can be used as a starting point for those keen to learn about these snakes and how to keep them. The second is to provide a comprehensive reference for those who already have knowledge of keeping reticulated pythons.

This book aims to provide you with all of the information that you need to be able to prepare yourself for keeping a reticulated python. However, that is not to say that by reading this book you will be prepared to care for these snakes – you should do your own research and get as much experience with reticulated pythons as you can.

The internet provides many sources of information regarding reticulated pythons. This is a good place for doing further reading and research, although you will have to judge the reliability of the information for yourself. After reading this book continue learning about reticulated pythons and look to combine this information with your own experience – as reptile keepers we should always look to improve the way we care for our animals.

In the UK it is legal to purchase and move reticulated pythons. This may not be the case in all countries and it is your responsibility to be aware of any relevant laws in your country.

The name 'reticulated python' is often abbreviated by keepers to 'retic' (pronounced ree-tic) and this book will use the term throughout.

Every effort has been made to identify and contact the copyright holder of each picture. If you see a picture that belongs to you but has been otherwise credited, please email me at thesid2k@hotmail.com.

About the Author

I'm an enthusiastic keeper of reticulated pythons and other exotic animals – I have loved snakes for as long as I can remember. My interest in all things related to wildlife started early and has focused on cold-blooded animals, specifically snakes. I was trusted with my first at the age of 10 and bought myself a beautiful corn snake hatchling with my birthday money – a snake that is now aged 23 and still with me today.

Having always loved boas it wasn't until my wife bought a reticulated python for herself that I began to really appreciate these wonderful creatures. I was captivated by how alert and active they are, especially when this alertness and activity are exhibited in such large snakes. I now love reticulated pythons and think they're amazing animals, and I know that a lot of people who keep them agree with me.

In addition to many years of keeping snakes, I have spent countless hours reading, learning and gathering information about reticulated pythons from many different sources. I hope that through this book I will be able to share my passion for reticulated pythons with you, and provide a useful resource about them for both new and experienced keepers alike.

I am on the committee of my local reptile group – Portsmouth Reptiles and Amphibian Society (PRAS) in the UK – which is a group of like-minded animal enthusiasts. A lot of the club activities involve educating people about animals and encouraging responsible keeping of reptiles and amphibians. As a club we receive a lot of animals in need of rehoming due to owners not fully researching or being prepared for the longevity of care needed for some reptiles.

The three reticulated pythons that my wife and I own feature throughout this book. Chaos is a male Dwarf reticulated python that was bred by UK Exotics in 2013 – he is a very calm snake and is often excited to get out of his enclosure only to fall asleep on the sofa. Envy is a female Tiger reticulated python that was bred by Imperial Retics in 2015 – she is very active and her first thought is always for food. Fury is our youngest. He is a male albino bred by Imperial Retics in 2015 – he is our most nervous retic and is scared of his own tail.

▼ *Envy, yearling tiger retic. Picture credit: Natasha James*

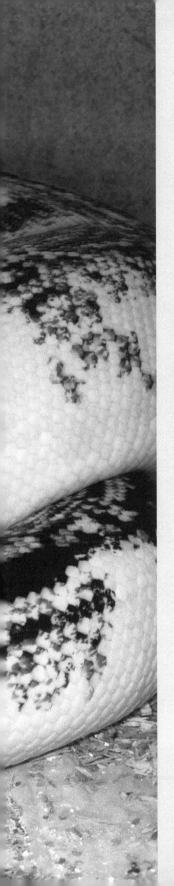

CHAPTER 1

IDENTIFICATION AND CHARACTERISTICS OF RETICS

Picture credit: Anne and Thierry

Scientific names, classification and taxonomy

Under the system for classifying all living things that was developed by Swedish botanist Carolus Linnaeus in the mid-1700s, the reticulated python – *Malayopython reticulatus* (previously *Python reticulatus* as well as other names) – belongs to the class of Reptilia. This class consists of turtles, lizards, snakes and crocodilians, which are characterised by being endothermic or cold-blooded, i.e. they require environmental temperatures to moderate their body temperature.

Reticulated pythons belong to the suborder of Serpents and the family of *Pythonidae*, which are non-venomous snakes originating from Africa, Asia and Australia and are closely related to the *Boidae* family, which includes boas. There are 31 species within the *Pythonidae* family and a number of subspecies that are recognised as being part of it.

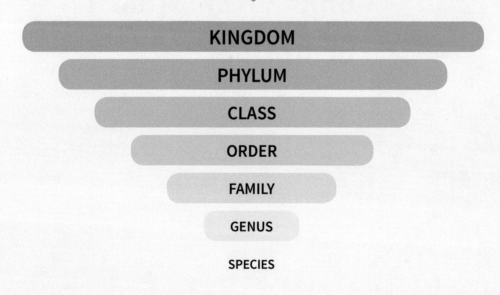

Hierarchy of biological classification

under which all live organisms are classified

KINGDOM

PHYLUM

CLASS

ORDER

FAMILY

GENUS

SPECIES

Families are further divided into smaller groups known as genera (genus for singular), which contain animals with very similar features that are closely related. There are currently eight genera within the *Pythonidae* family. The reticulated python belongs to the *Python* genus (often called 'true pythons'). This genus includes other commonly kept species including the Burmese (*Python bivittatus*), Royal (*Python regius*) and Blood pythons (*Python brongersmai*).

There are three distinct subspecies of reticulated python:
- *M. reticulatus reticulatus*
- *M. reticulatus jampeaneus* (a Dwarf subspecies)
- *M. reticulatus saputrai* (a Dwarf subspecies)

The two subspecies – *saputrai* and *jampeaneus* – were re-classed as separate subspecies in 2002 (Auliya et al, 2002). It is thought that there are a number of other wild populations of reticulated pythons that could also be categorised as subspecies.

These subspecies and proposed subspecies are strongly linked to the specific locations where these snakes originated. Reticulated python populations that have lived in isolated locations – islands in particular – have evolved different characteristics from retics in other places. For example, the two subspecies described by Auliya et al are generally smaller than *M. reticulatus reticulatus* and are considered as Dwarf retics.

Basic anatomy – description, lifespan and size

Reticulated pythons are slender and lean-bodied snakes relative to their length, and are characterised by their distinct reticulated (meaning 'constructed, arranged or marked like a net') patterning along their back and sides.

▶ *Adult female with classic wild-type patterning. Picture credit: Scott Cochrane of SC Pythons*

◄ ▲ *Chaos, a juvenile retic with classic wild-type markings showing black patterning and iridescence in natural sunlight, with silver sides and white rosettes. Picture credit: Natasha James*

The normal colouration is black reticulations over orange, green or brown base colours across the back, with a cream or light grey belly and sides that are silver or grey with white rosettes surrounded by black outlines. However, the natural pattern and colouration of retics can be very variable between snakes – some of which may be due to the specific location where it (or its ancestors) originated or due to selective breeding in captivity.

There is very little visual difference between male and female reticulated pythons, although females tend to get slightly larger than males when fully grown. Retics will have nearly achieved their full adult size by five years of age, although they will continue to grow for several more years.

Longest species in the world

Retics are one of the largest species of snake and are generally considered to be the longest species, while green anacondas are considered to be the heaviest. People have a fascination with large snakes and stories from early explorers captured their imaginations. This interest has persisted throughout the years with zoos and private collectors paying huge sums of money for large specimens that they can show off to the public, with some well-known snakes being Colossus, Cassius, Samantha, Atomic (Big) Betty and Medusa – who holds the Guinness World Record for the longest snake in captivity at 7.67m (25ft 2in).

In the early 1900s a reward of $1000 was offered for a live, healthy snake that measured over 9.1m (30ft) in length. It was first proposed by President Theodore Roosevelt and has been updated several times over the years and was raised to $50,000 in 1980 by the Wildlife Conservation Society (previously the New York Zoological Society), but no claim for the reward has ever been made.

Retics can grow to over 6.1m (20ft) in length, although not all are likely to reach such huge sizes. Specimens from some locations are considered Dwarf or Super Dwarf retics and can stay as small as 1.8–2.4m (6–8ft) in length. It is generally only the retics that inhabit the mainland and larger islands in Southeast Asia that are capable of growing to lengths in excess of 6.1m (20ft). The majority do not exceed 6.1m (20ft), and it is estimated that only around one percent of retics grow to be larger than this.

▶ *A 6.96m (22ft 10in) reticulated python, shot by Kekek Aduanan on the right, on 9 June 1970 on the island of Luzon, the Philippines. Picture credit: Janet Headland (SIL International)*

▲ *Examples of large retics including Rosie (top left) who measures 6.6m (21ft 8in).*
Picture credit: Steve Dawson

Some reports of very large retics and other snakes have been disproved, either by more experienced herpetologists or a more accurate measurement after death (Barker et al, 2012). Some of the largest retics that are thought to be reliably measured include one that was kept on display in a zoo in Thailand during the 1990s that measured 7.06m (23ft 2in), a female in a Malaysian zoo measuring 6.93m (22ft 9in) and a wild retic in East Kalimantan, Borneo, Indonesia, documented in a paper by Fredriksson in 2005 that scientists measured under anaesthetic at 6.91m (22ft 8in).

It may be that there are a handful of undiscovered retics in the wild that exceed 7.0m (23ft) in length, and perhaps it is possible for some to reach 7.3m (24ft), but it seems unlikely that any could reach 9.1m (30ft) due to the availability of suitably sized food. If such a snake did exist, it truly would be one of a kind. Ultimately any retic close to or over 6.1m (20ft) in length is a very large and impressive animal and should be respected as such.

▲ *The impressive size and girth of a 10 year old, 5.5m (18ft) female retic.*
Picture credit: Nelson Jacobson

Retics in the wild: distribution, habitat, threats and lifestyle

Reticulated pythons are naturally found throughout Southeast Asia, including Indonesia and surrounding islands, from Thailand and surrounding countries in the north to Timor in the south. They are the most widely distributed of all the python species and there is considerable variation in their appearance and genetics, depending on what part of Southeast Asia they or their ancestors are from. Retics are often described by their location or that of their ancestors, e.g. Sumatra or Bali retics.

Conditions across mainland Southeast Asia are tropical and temperatures are generally hot (25–30°C/77–86°F) with high levels of rainfall all year round, especially during monsoon seasons, where annual rainfall can be more than 1,500mm (59in). The seasons are broadly May–September for the Southwest monsoon, and October–January for the Northeast monsoon, which generally brings the most rain.

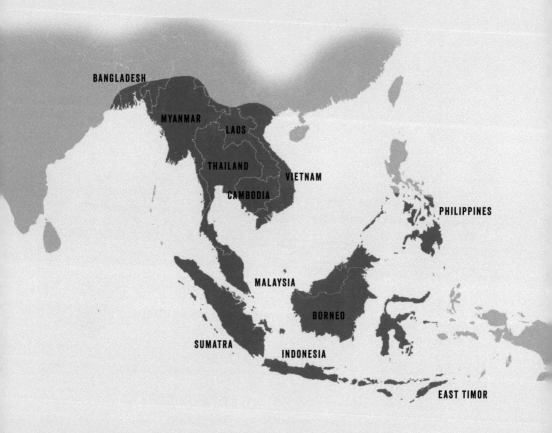

▲ *Retics are distributed across Southeast Asia, from Thailand to Timor.*

▲ *The tropical jungles of Southeast Asia offer retics an ideal habitat.*

► *Young wild retic.*

Conditions across the islands and archipelagos of Southeast Asia are similar with hot temperatures and high levels of rainfall all year round. Again there are two seasons based on the monsoons, but the frequency and quantity of rainfall varies across the region and between seasons.

Retics normally inhabit warm and humid tropical rain forests, although they have been known to adapt to urban locations and do well there. These warm and humid habitats provide ideal conditions for retics, which allows them to thermoregulate, keeps their skin in good condition and provides a climate that supports lots of other species that they can feed on.

◀ *Retic perched in the branch of a tree.*

▼ *Chaos having a stretch on the grass. Picture credit: Natasha James*

Small retics are very agile and will often climb and spend time in trees; this behaviour is good for avoiding predators, such as birds, wild cats and other mammals, and allows them to hunt a wider range of prey. As they get larger they are often found nearer ground level as very little will predate on a large retic, although they are still able to climb and hunt in trees. Retics are strong swimmers and are known to spend long periods of time submerged with only the top of their heads above water, waiting for prey.

In the wild, retics are hunted for their skin and the pet trade. Official Convention on International Trade in Endangered Species (CITES) quotas for 2017 show that around 160,000 snakes were legally allowed to be captured in the wild from Indonesia and Malaysia for the leather industry in Indonesia. In addition, 6,000 were allowed to be captured and exported live, which mostly went to private keepers and the pet trade. This level of harvesting has been going on for at least the past 16 years and has been described as unsustainable by some experts (Shine et al, 1998). This, combined with the decline of their habitat, means that they are becoming more endangered in the wild, with some localised populations being decimated.

Retics are often feared and persecuted throughout their range as a source of food and a potential threat to human life. Many people will kill them and other snakes when encountered. However, there have only been a handful of recorded cases of human deaths by retics both in the wild and in captivity. It is important to stress that retics are large, powerful snakes, but these incidents are very rare and relatively speaking they pose less danger than many large wild and domesticated animals, including dogs and horses (Hospital Episode Statistics, England and Wales, 2015).

The diet of a retic in the wild will consist of almost anything that they can overpower and swallow. For hatchlings this will consist of mice, rats, small lizards, birds and amphibians, while for adults their diet includes larger prey items such as deer, wild pigs and monkeys.

Like all snakes they eat their prey whole – they are able to dislocate their jaws and have very elastic skin and tendons that allows them to eat prey items that are much larger than their head and wider than the widest part of their body. Retics have been reported

▼ *Retic skin used in the leather industry*

to consume items up to one quarter of the snake's length and weighing as much as the animal itself. They have been recorded eating wild pigs that weight around 60kg (132lb) and there is a documented case of a retic eating a 29kg (64lb) sun bear (Fredriksson, 2005).

Unlike many other large constrictors, retics are active hunters that use their lean and muscular bodies to hunt in trees, on the ground and in water. They are also opportunists and will eat whenever they can, which means that in the wild there is often little predictability between their meals. It has been observed that retics are able to adapt to living in close proximity to humans, where small and medium-sized specimens sustain themselves on a diet that is dominated by rats and domestic poultry (Shine et al, 1998.).

Like other large snakes, adult retics can go for a long time between meals with some being recorded as not eating for over a year. Hatchlings and young snakes in general will eat more frequently than adults. As young snakes they have relatively fast metabolisms and can digest a meal in two–five days. When fed large amounts of prey they are able to grow very rapidly – some people have reported hatchlings reaching 2.4–3.0m (8–10ft) in length within their first year.

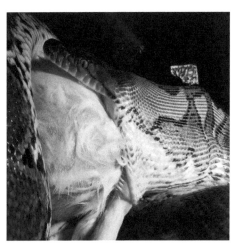

◀ *Adult retic eating a large food item. Picture Credit: Mystic Genetics*

▼ *A wild retic in Thailand photographed after eating a large prey item*

► Close up of Envy.
Picture credit: Natasha
James

Retics in Captivity

Reticulated pythons have been kept in captivity for many years, although prior to 1980–1990 retics in captivity were rare and mostly limited to zoos and other collections for display rather than as pets. One of the most famous early captive retics was Colossus, who was kept in Pittsburgh Zoo, Pennsylvania, USA, which at the time was called Highland Park Zoo. Colossus lived there throughout the 1950s and died in April 1963. Other large snakes that were kept in zoos include Samantha at the Bronx Zoo in the 1980s, Cassius at Knaresborough Zoo in North Yorkshire, UK, and Atomic (Big) Betty at the Australian Reptile Park, Somersby, New South Wales.

During the 1980s, reticulated pythons started to become popular in the pet trade in Europe and the US, with a lot of snakes being caught in the wild, most likely from Sumatra, Sulawesi and Thailand. These snakes were often caught as juveniles and would have been held in holding enclosures in Indonesia before being exported to pet shops around the world. They would then be purchased by private collectors and kept in sub-optimal conditions, given that keepers at that time did not have sufficient experience to know how to best care for them.

It is hardly surprising that early wild-caught (WC) retics got a reputation for being very hard to work with and for having an aggressive nature. It is more likely that these snakes were actually showing nervousness and defensive behaviour due to being taken out of the wild and put into captivity in close proximity to humans.

Throughout the 1990s with increased numbers of captive-bred snakes over multiple generations combined with improvements to retic husbandry, the reputation for being aggressive seems to have gone, and many captive-bred retics can become used to regular

◄ *An adult Tiger retic eating a large rat.*
Picture credit: Jason Bert

handling without showing any sign of aggression or nervousness. They can live for around 30 years in captivity (20–25 years in the wild), similar to many large python species.

In captivity, retics are commonly fed on pre-killed rodents including rats and mice, and also rabbits that have been bred specifically for food that are frozen and thawed before feeding. Other pre-killed food items can be used, including larger animals such as piglets, goats, calves, lambs, chickens and turkeys. Given the slow metabolism of snakes, it is possible to over-feed retics, which can lead to obesity and long-term health problems, as with many other snake species.

In the pet trade, just as in the wild, retics range in sizes from 1.8–2.4m (6–8ft) to over 6.1m (20ft). There are several factors that influence the size of retics, including the location that they or their ancestors originated from, the individual genetics of the parents and their diet. Retics from different locations are often grouped into 'Mainland', 'Dwarf' and 'Super Dwarf' based on the size that they are likely to reach. However, it is never possible to guarantee that they will grow to their expected size.

In captivity, retics from different localities are regularly bred together and mixed, so while it is possible to find examples from specific localities from trusted breeders, in some cases there is little or no indication about where the snake's ancestors may have originated. These mixed breedings are unlikely to occur in the wild due to the isolated locations of many retic populations, however in captivity it is done to get favourable genetic mutations (such as colour and pattern morphs) and/or to selectively breed retics to influence their size. As such, when buying one be aware that some labelled as Dwarf or Super Dwarf may have genes from much larger snakes in their DNA, which could lead to a snake that exceeds the expected size for a Dwarf or Super Dwarf.

▲ *Clockwise from top left: Orange Ghost Stripe (OGS) Golden Child. Picture credit: Anne and Thierry. Platinum Motley Tiger. Picture credit: Anne and Thierry. Purple Motley. Picture credit: Scott Cochrane of SC Pythons. Golden Child, Sunfire and Tiger. Picture credit: Scott Cochrane of SC Pythons*

Many colour and pattern variations are available in retics, which are generally due to specific genetic traits that are selectively bred into the snakes to produce an altered colour or pattern in the offspring; some common examples include Tiger and Albino. These genetic traits are generally referred to as favourable mutations or morphs. They often come from wild-caught snakes that are found to have an unorthodox colour or pattern, and then selectively line-bred in captivity to replicate this appearance. Multiple morphs can be bred into individual retics, which is the same as with many commonly kept captive-bred reptiles.

Due to their size variation, the colour and pattern distinction and their active and inquisitive nature, reticulated pythons can make excellent pets and display animals, providing that their care requirements can be met throughout their lives. While retics can be very rewarding snakes to keep, they are a long-term responsibility and you need to do your research and ensure that you are able to care for and safely handle a large snake.

CHAPTER 2

CHOOSING A RETICULATED PYTHON

Picure credit: Raul Garcia

Is a reticulated python the right snake for you?

This snake certainly won't be for everyone, just like a dog or a cat isn't for everyone. Large adults require a large space, a lot of heating and sizable food items. You should consider:

● Whether you can afford to provide the space, heating and food for a snake that could live for 25–30 years.
● The practicality of managing a potentially large snake – for example, are you able to handle it safely for both yourself and the animal?
● Do you have access to a veterinary practice that specialises in exotic animals?
● Can you provide the regular maintenance to keep your retic in good condition and do you have someone willing to look after your snake if you go away?

If you are considering keeping a retic it is recommended to locate and research the vets in your area who specialise in reptiles. In particular you may want to talk to a veterinary practice to ensure they would be able to treat a retic should the need arise – not all vets will be willing to deal with a large retic in distress – even if they do have some experience of dealing with smaller, more common exotic species.

Retics are amazing snakes – they are more active, alert and inquisitive than many commonly kept species. The majority have a very even temperament, without showing any signs of aggressive or defensive behaviour, and with a lot of time and effort they

▼ *A beautiful Amaretto Motley retic. Picture credit: Karl Emery*

▲ *When looking at hatchlings you need to consider whether you can accommodate an adult retic.*
Picture credit: Matthew Genser

can become very easy and rewarding to handle. This, combined with the fact that they are relatively straightforward to maintain, can make them an excellent species to keep whether you are looking for a pet or an animal to display.

If you are careful and purchase a retic from a reliable breeder, it is possible to get a Super Dwarf that will mature at around 1.8–2.4m (6–8ft) in length when fully grown. This will provide all the fun and interest of owning a retic but in a somewhat smaller snake instead of one that could potentially reach 6.1m (20ft) in size. You could also get a retic with natural colour and pattern or with a genetic mutation (morph) that alters the colour and/or pattern. With the morphs that are available it is possible to get almost patternless white or black retics, or one with very complex patterning and colours of orange, yellow, purple, grey, brown and gold.

Retics are being captive bred in large numbers, which means they are being sold to a wider range of keepers than ever before. Some of these keepers are not prepared for or able to manage one properly. This means that rescue and rehoming centres are starting to be given retics by owners that do not have the time, patience or resources to look after it. If you are new to retics please do as much research as possible to prepare yourself for a snake that may be with you for around 25 years or longer, and make sure you are not one of the people having to rehome your retic later in its life. If you are an experienced keeper and willing to get a retic that may have an unknown background or temperament you may wish to consider looking to get one from a rehoming centre.

Getting some experience

Keeping other snake species will give you some experience of setting up a suitable environment for a reptile as well as the basic skills for caring for a retic. However, it is important to note that keeping a corn snake, a royal python or even a boa constrictor will not fully prepare you for keeping a retic. They are alert, always looking for food, lean and powerful snakes that even at small sizes can be intimidating to some people.

If you think that a retic is for you, it is strongly recommended that you get some hands-on experience first. If you are totally new to snakes then this is especially important and it would be worth getting some experience of retics of all sizes and ages. If you have some experience with other snakes then it is perhaps more important to get some familiarity with adults retics to develop a feel for their size and strength. It is worth contacting someone with adult retics through a local reptile group, shop, breeder or friend and ask them if you

▼ *A Lemonglow retic. Picture credit: Darren Elson*

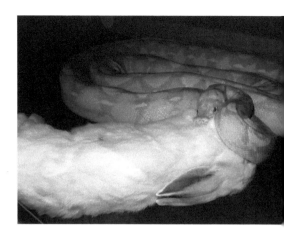
► *Large retics will need large food such as rabbits. Picture credit: Scott Cochrane of SC Pythons*

could get some hands-on experience of the following three aspects of retic husbandry – although not necessarily all at the same time:

Getting the retic in and out of the enclosure – this is particularly useful as it may introduce you to 'tap training' (covered in chapter 4) and give you an idea of how a retic may react to being disturbed, including their feeding response. It is important to experience the size and power of an adult retic and getting them in and out of the enclosure is one of the more awkward parts of handling one. A retic that doesn't want to come out or go back into its enclosure can be a real handful. First-hand experience of this will be much more beneficial than someone just handing a retic to you to hold.

Feeding a retic – it can be intimidating to feed a large snake, so it is a good idea to do so in the company of an experienced keeper before you buy one. This should show you the feeding response of the snake and help you understand how to feed it safely and what to keep in mind to stay safe.

Cleaning out after it has defecated – while this may sound silly, it is a messy and unpleasant task and best to encounter it before you buy your own retic so that you know what to expect, as eating large food items means leaving a large mess. Retics are relatively messy snakes that urinate and defecate regularly – more regularly than boa constrictors, for example – so make sure you can face doing this frequently.

If you can find somewhere or someone willing to let you do all of these things before buying a retic it will eliminate some of the surprises that you might find as a keeper, as well as giving you a chance to ask yourself, 'Am I able to cope with this on a regular basis?' If the answer is 'no', that's okay – retics won't be for everyone and at least you have found out before buying one.

▲ *A beautiful Super Motley Platinum Sunfire Tiger, thought to be the world's first, bred by Anne and Thierry. Picture credit: Anne and Thierry*

At this stage you may ask yourself whether a smaller retic is the right option. If so, you could think about getting a Dwarf or Super Dwarf and maybe buying a male rather than a female, as they tend to stay smaller. If a retic is sold as a Dwarf or Super Dwarf it is important to make sure you trust the seller and that the snake is a true Dwarf or Super Dwarf and unlikely to grow too large, but even then there are no guarantees that it won't grow to be larger than expected.

Buying a hatchling retic is often suggested as a way to give new keepers experience of keeping retics – this will give you a chance to get used to feeding, handling, cleaning out and keeping the snake so that as it grows in size, you grow in experience. This is particularly good for letting you learn the individual snake's temperament and to learn to read its body language, such as whether it is feeling threatened or looking for food, etc. This will give you and the animal a chance to get to know each other and for the snake to gain trust in you and not feel threatened when being handled. Getting bitten by a baby retic is a lot more forgiving than getting bitten by an adult!

Buying a reticulated python

When buying a snake it is important to look for a healthy specimen, whether it is a hatchling or an adult. It is useful to note that retics generally go through some colour change as they grow, as well as some daily colour changes in terms of becoming darker or lighter, so you may want to get an idea of what the adult will look like before getting a hatchling.

You will want to be confident that the snake is feeding and shedding well, since these are often an early indication of ill health. It is especially important with baby snakes to make sure that they are feeding regularly because sometimes hatchlings are weak and will have difficulty feeding. Young snakes should shed within 14 days of hatching and should not be fed before this. Once they have fed several times they will usually continue to eat on a regular basis. Many breeders will keep records of a hatchling's diet and shedding as it lets a potential owner see their routines. It is unlikely that an adult will come with feeding records, but as a potential buyer it doesn't hurt to ask and as a keeper it is worth maintaining records for your own animals.

Many breeders and shops will be happy to courier a purchased snake to you, but if you are inexperienced it is worth seeing and handling it before you buy so you can assess the animal's general condition. Check to make sure the eyes are clear and look healthy – the eyes are also a good place to check for mites, which will often try to embed themselves just under the edge of the eye scales. Check that the cloaca – the posterior orifice on the underside of the snake before the tail – is clean and doesn't look blocked and that the owner can confirm that it has been defecating regularly. Try to listen to the breathing to give an indication that the airways and lungs are clear and healthy – you want to make sure you cannot hear anything that sounds like a blockage, gurgling or wheezing. Have a look at the general condition of the scales and make sure you cannot see any stuck skin from previous sheds, as that could be a sign the snake isn't shedding properly.

▶ *Beautiful Motley Tiger hatchling. Picture credit: Scott Cochrane of SC Pythons*

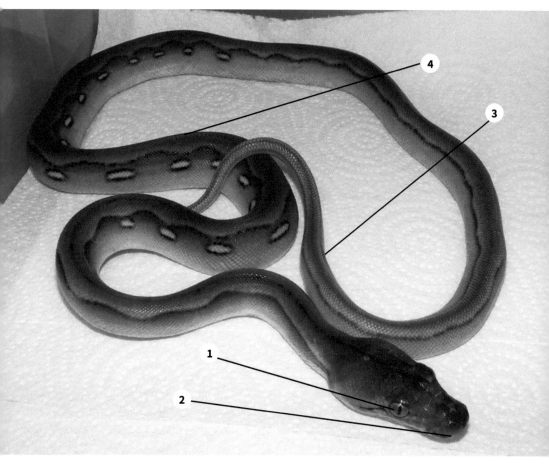

▲ *A hatching female suntiger retic.* **1** *Eyes – check to see they look clear and healthy with no signs of mites.* **2** *Airways – check for blockages around nostrils and mouth, and that the breathing doesn't sound laboured or blocked.* **3** *Cloaca – check it is clean.* **4** *Overall – check the condition of the skin and whether there is any sign of stuck shed. Picture credit: Scott Cochrane of SC Pythons*

If buying a hatchling, check the snake's parents if possible – look at the size and condition of them. Knowing the size of the parents is especially important if you are buying a retic that is a Dwarf or Super Dwarf because this will help you judge the adult size of your snake as the genetics of the parents play a major role in determining this. There are no guarantees, but giving yourself as much information as possible will offer the best chance of knowing the size you can expect when the snake matures.

Some breeders will supply their snakes with some form of paperwork. This is their guarantee to show what genes the snake has – it will often include information about whether the snake is from a Dwarf or Super Dwarf line, or whether they carry certain genetic morphs. This will help you to know what you can expect as your snake grows and/ or breeds, but again there are no guarantees.

When you get a new retic, or indeed any snake, there are several steps that you should take to reduce stress on your animal and help it to settle into its new environment:

● If you have a lot of other snakes or reptiles, consider setting up the enclosure in isolation to reduce the chance of any disease or parasites transferring to your other animals.
● Put the snake in its enclosure – which has been set up as appropriate in advance of getting your retic – with as little handling as possible. Many snakes will be extremely nervous and may show defensive behaviour at this stage, including a defensive strike; this is especially true for baby snakes that haven't learnt that humans are not a threat.
● If the enclosure is in a busy area of your house you may consider covering it with a blanket or towel for a couple of days so that the snake cannot see movement.
● For the first week do not handle your retic if possible and only go into the enclosure to change water and clean up any mess.
● After a week, offer a food item slightly smaller than normal for the size of the snake, for example if your new retic would usually eat a small weaner rat (a very young rat) which are usually around 25-30g, consider trying to feed a rat fluff (a baby rat that has just started getting fur) or small adult mouse which will usually weigh around 15-20g. This is because stress often affects a snake's digestive system and can lead to food items being regurgitated, although this is less of an issue with retics since they have very strong feeding responses.
● Two days after feeding, or when the snake has defecated, you can begin to handle it. Initially this should be short and infrequent sessions – for example, you could start picking it up on some of the occasions when you change the water.
● As you build trust with your retic so that it starts to recognise that you are not a threat and can distinguish you from food, you can increase the duration and frequency with which you handle your snake.

CHAPTER 3

SET-UP FOR A
RETICULATED PYTHON

What enclosure to use

There is no right or wrong set-up for a retic, providing you can meet your snake's requirements and it remains healthy. Your choice will be based on your personal preference regarding appearance and practicality. The majority of keepers prefer to keep their snake in fairly minimalistic enclosures – i.e. a vivarium, on paper with a water bowl and a couple of hides. This style of set up has been proven to work well and allow retics to live healthy lives because is easy to keep clean and hygienic while maintaining stable temperatures and humidity.

While large, naturalistic enclosures are possible it becomes more difficult to maintain the correct temperature and humidity, which can be detrimental to the snake's health. It can also make some snakes difficult to handle – some will become nervous in a large space if there is not sufficient cover or hides. The snake may also become less accessible if they can anchor themselves to branches or other decor. For these reasons some breeders will advocate that large natural-looking enclosures are not good for retics; however, if you are able to overcome these issues then a large naturalistic set-up can provide an excellent home.

Before going into the main content of this chapter, here are two very important points about the set-up:

● Retics should never be kept together in the same enclosure. In the wild they are solitary animals – males will fight each other and can cause fatal injuries with their teeth, especially during breeding season when they search and compete for females. Keeping retics in the same enclosure, even two females, risks the health of the animals through fighting, possible feeding injuries and the spread of disease.

● Make sure that your enclosure is fully set up with stable conditions before introducing a retic or indeed any snake. This will minimise stress and allow the snake to settle properly.

Below are some common choices of enclosures for retics along with advantages and disadvantages for each. The extent of the set-up will depend greatly on the snake itself: its size, age and genetics.

◄ An Albino retic in an attractive naturalistic set-up. Picture credit: David van Berlo

▲ *A Really Useful Box (RUB) can make a good enclosure for a retic hatchling with hides and a water bowl.*

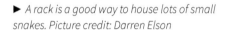

▶ *A rack is a good way to house lots of small snakes. Picture credit: Darren Elson*

Plastic tubs

A lot of people keep hatchlings and young retics in plastics tubs, which if needed can be kept in racks containing multiple tubs. This is especially common with breeders who have a large number of hatchlings at the same time. Plastic tubs can be very practical in that they are available in a large range of shapes and sizes, and are generally cheap and easy to keep clean. It is more difficult to find plastic tubs large enough for adult retics, but it is possible to find custom racks with large plastic tub draws. It is important to make sure that the plastic tub has sufficient ventilation – usually some air holes can be drilled in the sides – and that the lid is secure with clips or locks to stop the snake from escaping.

Wooden vivariums

A vivarium – often referred to as a viv – is an enclosure that is enclosed on all sides except the front, which is glass or plastic that opens along runners or hinges. Wooden vivariums are generally made of laminated chipboard or painted/sealed plywood on the back, sides, top and bottom with glass sliding doors at the front.

Wooden vivariums are commonly available for reptiles, and many shops or suppliers will be able to provide custom-made ones to suit all sizes, including vivariums that can house large retics. They come in a wide range of colours and styles and it is easy to secure heating equipment inside them.

Wooden vivariums may need to be sealed along the joining edges to cope with high humidity, retic urine and water bowls that frequently get tipped over. This can be done with pond paint, aquarium sealant or other sealants safe for animals and will make your vivarium easier to clean and last longer.

▲ A 1.8m (6ft) wooden vivarium.

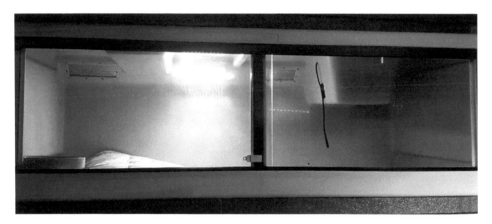
▲ A plastic vivarium set-up. Picture credit: Scott Cochrane of SC Pythons

Plastic vivariums

These offer similar benefits to wooden vivariums and do not require sealing as the plastic will not get damaged by water and humidity. Plastic vivariums are easier to clean and are longer lasting than wooden examples. They are also lighter in weight, which makes them more practical for moving around. Plastic vivariums can be expensive, but are arguably worth the investment for a snake that could live over 20 years.

Other

It is also worth mentioning glass aquariums and terrariums as retic enclosures. One made of glass can be used for retics (especially hatchlings) but it is important to consider how to provide the correct heating and that there is a secure lid so that the snake cannot escape. Glass enclosures are generally not that common for retics and are not discussed further in this book, however if you choose to use one then ensure it can provide the same conditions as described in the rest of this chapter.

This table provides details on a number of aspects for different types of enclosure:

	Plastic tubs	Wooden vivariums	Plastic vivariums
Cost	Very cheap	Mid-priced	Relatively expensive
Availibility	Easily available from general stores and online.	Easily available from pet shops and online.	Uncommon in pet shops, but available to order online.
Sizes	Many sizes available for young/small retics. Little to no sizes available that would house large retics.	Many sizes available. Larger vivariums may need to be custom ordered.	Many sizes available – may need to be custom ordered.
Appearance	Not visually attractive. Unable to easily view retic.	Allows good viewing from the front.	Allows good viewing from the front.
Security	Plastics tubs with lid clips are widely available.	Easy to attach a lock or use wedges.	Often available with built-in locks.
Durability	Long lasting.	Wood can warp or become damaged by moisture and humidity. Recommended to seal the vivarium for use over a long period.	Long lasting.
Cleaning	Easy to clean. Easily able to move the tub.	Easy to clean, especially if the vivarium is sealed. Can be heavy to move.	Easy to clean.
Heating	Can be difficult to achieve correct heating gradient if tub is kept in a room with low or changeable temperatures. Not always easy to mount an overhead heat source.	Efficient, since wood is a good insulator of heat. Easy to mount overhead heat source.	Easy to mount overhead heat source. Often built to specification with heat plate/heat panel already fitted.
Humidity	Good for maintaining humidity.	Generally good at retaining humidity.	Generally good at retaining humidity.
Other comments		Easy to attach decor to customise, e.g. branches or a shelf.	

Size of enclosure

Given the huge range of sizes that retics can reach and that they can grow from a 60cm (23in) hatchling to a 6.1m+ (20ft+) giant, it is very difficult to define size requirements for the enclosure. Here are some common guidelines that are often given as advice to keepers, and some discussion around these.

'Bigger is better' and 'There is no minimum enclosure size': This is very much true – retics are active snakes compared to many other large species – and the more space you can provide the more space it will use. If you find yourself wondering what size enclosure to get, get the biggest that you can fit in your house.

'Ensure that the snake does not feel exposed': Some keepers will claim that this means retics should not be kept in very large enclosures, and especially not to put babies into one. It is common among many snake species that if you put them in a large space where they might feel exposed this can cause them stress or make them display defensive behaviour and sometimes stop eating. While retics seem less fazed by being put in large open spaces than many species, it is still important to make sure the snake does not feel exposed. This is not to say don't put the snake in a large vivarium. However, if you do put a small retic into a large space, make sure that there are plenty of places for it to hide, lots of decor to provide cover and give it time to adjust.

'Adult retics can be suitably kept in a vivarium that is 2.4 x 1.2m (8 x 4ft) – length x depth – except only the very largest females': While not all retics will get large, if you have a Mainland you should be prepared to provide an enclosure that is 2.4 x 1.2m (8 x 4ft), although you may wish to consider a larger space. That is not to say that all retics will attain large sizes and it is possible for smaller adults to be comfortably housed in modest enclosures, but any extra space you provide will not be wasted on these active snakes, as they will use all available space.

Judgement and pragmatism based on your individual snake should drive your decision for what enclosure size is suitable.

From hatchlings to adults

These guidelines will depend both on the size of the individual retic and the rate of growth – they will not be applicable to all snakes and so enclosure sizes, and growth stages should reflect the needs of the individual animal.

Hatchlings are likely to be content in a small plastic tub, aquarium or vivarium of around 30–60 litres or 0.6–0.9m (2–3ft) long for around the first 6–12 months, depending on growth rates. Given the speed that retics can grow, a relatively cheap enclosure might be a good option because it will outgrow it within a short space of time. Of course, this means the enclosure can then be cleaned out and used for other snakes.

Some people may move their retics straight to a large vivarium, but a midway point is probably sensible; this might consist of moving your snake to a tub around 70+ litres or a 1.2m (4ft) vivarium. This may remain suitable for a further one or two years, again depending on size and growth rate of the snake.

At this point a move to a final (or near final) enclosure should be suitable, and by this time you should have some idea of how large your retic is going to be once fully grown, based on its growth to this point. For example, if your retic is over 2.4m (8ft) and has outgrown a 1.2m (4ft) enclosure by 18 months then you have a snake that is likely to be a large adult and you will have to prepare for a large final enclosure.

As mentioned before, retics vary greatly in size so this information should only be used as a guide and your choices should be based on your animal and your circumstances.

▶ *Stack of 1.2m-long (4ft) plastic vivariums.*
Picture credit: Scott Cochrane of SC Pythons

► *A beautiful 3m (10ft) retic in a large enclosure. Picture credit: Derek Moore*

AUTHOR RECOMMENDATION – ENCLOSURES

● Start hatchings in suitably sized wooden vivarium or plastic tub.

● Move to a medium-sized vivarium or large plastic tub when needed.

● From there, upgrade to final adult vivarium with size dependent on the individual retic.

● Invest in a plastic vivarium for the final enclosure – it will last longer, is easier to clean and worth the money in the long run.

To note: If your retic escaped and you couldn't find it you should check any confined space including under objects such as sofa, and equally on top of things – you may be able to follow a trail of things that have been knocked over or moved. Small retics can fit through little gaps and have been known to get under floorboards and into walls and lofts – and possibly never be found. If you are unable to find your retic you could try leaving food out overnight to try and entice the snake from where it has been hiding. Although accidents can happen it is best to ensure your enclosure is secure and you supervise the snake at all times when handling it, even if you let it explore the area by itself.

Heating and temperatures

Coming from the tropical regions of Southeast Asia, retics need warm conditions, although not quite as hot as species from equatorial or desert locations. They are endothermic (cold-blooded) and like all reptiles they use the heat from their environment to control their body temperature. As such, it is important to provide a temperature gradient in the enclosure. This is usually achieved by using a heat source to create a hot end with somewhere to bask and a cooler end without heating.

Setting up a heat source so that the desired temperature for the hot end is met and allowing the heat to disperse to the other end of the enclosure is usually sufficient to provide a suitable gradient and achieve a good temperature for the cool end. However, if the enclosure is kept in a particularly cool place or is made of a material that does not insulate heat well, it may be necessary to add an additional heat source to make sure the temperature for the cool end is met.

Temperatures should be set up and monitored to ensure they are stable at the desired temperature before the retic is put into the enclosure. It is crucial that heat sources are guarded, are set up with a thermostat and temperatures are monitored using reliable thermometers – either digital or infrared are recommended.

The temperature ranges to aim for:
Hot end – 29°C (84°F) to 32°C (90°F)
Cool end – 24°C (76°F) to 27°C (80°F)

The temperatures above are given as a range because different keepers and breeders have had success keeping and breeding retics within those temperatures. As such, if you can maintain temperatures within this range and create a good gradient between the hot and cold end it should be suitable for your retic.

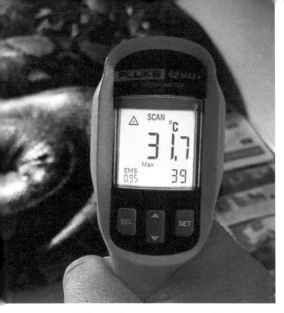

▲ An infrared thermometer measuring the warm side of a retic enclosure. Picture credit: Scott Cochrane of SC Pythons

▲ Ceramic heat bulb and guard attached to the top of a vivarium.

How to create the right temperature

All heating must be set up with a thermostat! This is a vital piece of equipment and is for the protection of the snake, the enclosure and wider surroundings. All heat sources must be set up with appropriate guards to prevent the snake coming into direct contact with the heat source. The most common cause of burns on snakes is from heating equipment that is not set up with a thermostat and guard.

Heat mats

These are commonly used for many reptiles including small retics. They are cheap to buy and run, and easy to set up. They can be used in vivariums or under plastic tubs. They are not recommended for large snakes, as the animal will not get an even distribution of heat all around its body due to heat mats only heating the surface area that they are in contact with. A heavy bodied snake sitting on a heat mat can cause thermal blocking and lead to burns to the skin. Thermal blocking is where the snake will be sat on the heat mat, trying to warm itself, but only its belly is getting heat which is unable to disperse evenly through the snake and could burn the snake's underside before the rest of the snake's body gets sufficient heat.

Heat mats provide very little ambient temperature so will not warm up the cool end of the enclosure. If the outside room temperature is low, a heat mat may mean that the cool end gets too cold, which can lead to incorrect humidity levels and health issues including respiratory infections.

Having said that, many breeders that have racking systems set up for a large number of plastic tubs use heat mats along the back of the rack. Due to the relatively small volume within each plastic tub and the large number of tubs close together, they are able to keep them in the correct range especially for breeders who generally have a higher ambient room temperature. This is a very efficient way to heat a large number of plastic tubs.

Heat lamps and ceramic bulbs

These are usually mounted on the top of the enclosure at the hot end and will provide concentrated heat to the area below the bulb as well as helping to provide ambient temperature to the rest of the enclosure. Bulbs are available in a large range of wattage and are easily installed in vivariums or suspended over plastic tubs depending on the type of lid. They can also be used in multiples if a wider hot spot or additional heating is needed.

Bulbs can get very hot and should be guarded – generally with a wire cage – at all times so that the snake cannot come into direct contact with it, which will cause burns. If you cannot hold your hand on the guard without it causing pain then it is too hot and the guard is not far enough away from the bulb.

Snakes can burn themselves on their heat source either just by climbing on them or by trying to gain additional heat if they are not sufficiently warm, which is why heat sources should always be covered by a guard.

Single bulbs – even 250W ceramic bulbs – may struggle to provide sufficient heat for a large enclosure, and the bulbs will either quickly burn out if they are on full power all the time or will leave the vivarium without sufficient heat. If the vivarium is in a room with a high ambient temperature a single bulb may be adequate to provide a hot spot at the hot end, while the room temperature is warm enough to keep the cool end at a suitable temperature. Alternatively it is possible to use a secondary heat source – for example multiple bulbs or a tube heater – to create the correct ambient temperatures and rely on the primary heat sources to provide the hot spot.

Reptile radiators/heat plates

Similar to heat bulbs, these need guarding since reptile radiators are made with ceramic elements. They are usually flat and can be attached to the top or side of the vivarium. They are more commonly used on large enclosures and are becoming increasingly popular.

Heat plates or heat panels function in a similar way to heat mats, but heat plates are made to radiate heat down or to the side. Some are designed for use inside the enclosure. Heat plates are usually able to provide sufficient heat to maintain the hot spot as well as ambient temperatures but are sometimes used to provide ambient temperatures as a secondary heat source. Similar to heat pads, these plates are long lasting and energy efficient.

► *A tube heater can be used to increase ambient temperatures within an enclosure.*

Tube heaters

Outside of reptile keeping, tube heaters are often used for places such as sheds, greenhouses and conservatories so are particularly suited to raising ambient temperatures in large areas. They are not ideal for creating a hot spot in a vivarium, but can be used in addition to a bulb to help maintain suitable ambient temperatures and make sure the cool end does not get too cold.

Thermostat (stat)

A thermostat is a device for controlling environmental temperatures when using a heat source, similar to your central heating. In this case, the environment is the snake's vivarium and the heat source is a bulb or reptile radiator. It is crucial that any heat source you use is controlled by a thermostat to provide stable temperatures. When setting up electrical equipment it is important to do so safely – if you have any uncertainty about your power supply or the heat source you are using then contact a professional electrician.

When using a thermostat the first thing to do is make sure it is compatible with the heat source you are using. You should check the wattage of your heat source and that the thermostat can work with this level of power – heat mats are often low wattage and some thermostats will not work with them. You should also check the thermostat type – there are three common types:

On/off thermostats – when the heat is too low the thermostat will turn the heat source on, and when the heat goes over the desired temperature the thermostat will turn it off. These are often used for heat mats.

Pulse proportional – rather than switching the heat source on and off like an on/off thermostat, a pulse stat will send power in waves. The speed of these will reflect how close to the correct temperature the heat source is – when the temperature is stable around the desired temperature it will pulse steadily. These are often used for ceramic bulbs and heaters.

Dimming – as the name suggests, a dimming stat will dim the heat source as it approaches the correct temperature, i.e. it will provide less power so the heat source is only partially on. This is often used for light-emitting heat sources and ceramic heaters.

Generally pulse and dimming thermostats are considered the best at maintaining the correct temperatures because there is less fluctuation compared to thermostats that turn the heat source on and off. Most ceramic bulbs or reptile radiators will work well with a pulse stat or a dimming stat. If you can invest in a dimming thermostat, this may be good as it has a wider range of uses if you want to use it for another type of set-up at a later stage.

There are four main parts to a thermostat:
1 Somewhere to plug the heat source into, rather than plugging the heat source into the mains.
2 A plug that should be connected to a mains socket (although don't turn it on until fully set up).
3 A sensor or probe that can read the temperature inside the vivarium and tell the stat whether it needs more or less heat to reach the desired temperature.
4 The dial or digital facing that is used to raise or lower the desired temperature.

◄ *A thermostat dial and cables to the sensor, mains plug and socket for the heat source to plug into.*

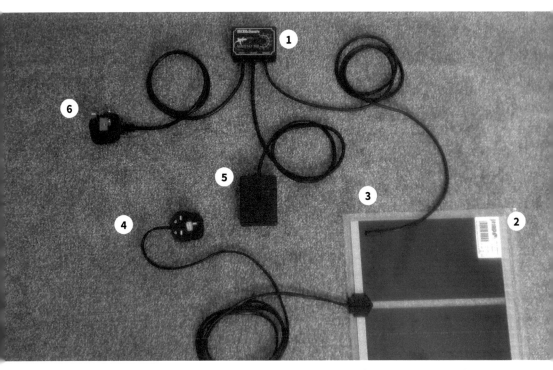

▲ *The layout of a thermostat set-up for a heat mat. This is the same for any heat source, other than the position of the thermostat probe.* **1** *Thermostat dial.* **2** *Heat mat.* **3** *Thermostat probe secured to the heat mat – a dab of superglue works well.* **4** *The heat mat is plugged into the socket on the thermostat.* **5** *Thermostat socket for the heat source.* **6** *The thermostat socket is plugged into the mains.*

The placement of the sensor is the most important part of setting up a thermostat. The sensor needs to be inside the vivarium, so you may need to drill a hole or feed the probe through a vent into the enclosure. It needs to be somewhere where the snake or decor will not block it from reading the temperature, i.e. not on the floor or behind a hide. It needs to be fixed in place so that the snake cannot move it, as that will affect the reading.

A good position for the probe in a vivarium, assuming you are using an overhead heat source at the hot end, is to run it along the back of the vivarium, directly in line with the heat source, and then fix the probe and cable in place so that the sensor is about 15cm (6in) from the floor and the snake cannot tangle or knock the cable or sensor. A good way to attach it is with cable clips in wooden vivariums or with a glue gun or dab of superglue in plastic tubs or vivariums.

With heat mats, glue is a good way to secure the sensor to the mat itself. With heat mats it is possible for the snake to sit directly on the sensor and affect the reading, which is another reason why they are not recommended for large retics.

◄ *For a heat bulb or ceramic bulb it is a good idea to secure the thermostat probe to the back of the enclosure using cable clips.*

Once the positioning and set-up of the thermostat is correct, turn the dial of the stat down to the minimum reading. The most reliable way to set temperatures is to use thermometers rather than reading from the thermostat dial. As such, place two thermometers inside the vivarium (digital ones are best here) with one in the hot end under the heat source and the other in the cool end to monitor the ambient temperature. Switch on the thermostat and let it adjust to the minimum setting – it may be that the setting is so low that the heat source does not even come on at this stage.

Going by the thermometer reading under the hot end and ignoring the numbers on the thermostat dial, gradually over several hours increase the temperature setting until the temperature inside the enclosure reaches the desired hot-end temperature.

At this point you need to make sure that the cool end is also within the desired range, then leave it for minimum of 24 hours to make sure the temperature is stable. Most digital thermometers will track the minimum and maximum temperature reached, so this will tell you whether it stays within the desired ranges.

At this point if the temperatures are not stable or reaching the desired level for both the hot and cool end, there are several things that could be an issue:

● The thermostat is turned up to max and the hot end is not reaching, or only just reaching, the right temperature – this may mean you need a more powerful heat source or a secondary heat source. If the heat source has to work hard and is on maximum power all the time it is likely that it will not last long before it needs to be replaced.

● The cool end is not sufficiently warm enough, which suggests that you may need to consider a secondary heat source to help with ambient temperatures.

● The temperatures vary a lot and/or the cool end is getting too hot, which suggests that the heat source is too strong for the size of the vivarium and you may want to consider a less powerful model or use it in a larger enclosure.

AUTHOR RECOMMENDATION – HEATING

● ALWAYS use a thermostat and ALWAYS guard the heat source

● Hot end: Try to aim for close to 29°C (84°F), but keep within the range of 29–32°C (84–90°F)

● Cool end: Try to aim for close to 24°C (76°F), but keep within the range of 24–27°C (76–80°F)

● Use an overhead heat source such a ceramic heater, reptile radiator or heat plate rather than a heat pad to ensure suitable ambient temperature.

● If your vivarium is in a room that reaches less than 20°C (68°F) then consider a second heat source to increase the ambient temperature and take some of the strain off the primary heat source.

Humidity

In the tropical climate of Southeast Asia, the humidity is often 70 percent and higher so achieving and maintaining a high humidity within your retic's vivarium is crucial for your snake in terms of shedding and overall health, particularly to prevent respiratory infections or other breathing problems.

Humidity refers to the level of evaporated water in the air, however things like ceramic heaters and changes in air temperature can affect it. Humidity levels can be measured with a hygrometer, which is equivalent to a thermometer reading the temperature. Digital hygrometers are generally superior to those with a dial, and they are cheap to buy and widely available.

In general you should aim for around 60–70 percent humidity. This can be increased during shed cycles to help your retic to shed its skin without issue. In most cases and most setups you should be able to achieve this – or close to it – by simply providing a large enough water bowl with sufficient surface area for water to evaporate to create humidity. However, if that is not sufficient here is a list of good ways to ensure that the humidity remains high in your retic's enclosure. You may find that you need to test several of these methods and monitor the humidity within your set-up before you find out what works best for you and your snake:

Have a large water bowl – this will provide a large surface area of water that will allow high levels of evaporation. This will also allow the snake to soak, which can aid with shedding –some retics seem to enjoy soaking even when they're not in shed. A secondary water bowl placed under the heat source could be used to boost humidity over a short period of time, but it is generally not recommended to keep a water bowl under the heat source as warm water is a good place for bacteria to grow.

Use substrate – the material that you use to line the bottom of the enclosure – that is good at retaining moisture and therefore increases humidity levels such as bark chips or aspen, rather than a substrate that does not hold humidity as well. Substrate is covered in more detail below.

Regularly spray the enclosure with water – perhaps once a day or more frequently when the snake is due to shed, which can be every four to six weeks.

Having a moist hide – this can be a lidded box with a hole cut in the side so that the snake can get in and out, and filled with damp or wet substrate – sphagnum moss is ideal. The box can then be placed inside the enclosure at the cool end, which can be used as a hide. A plastic tub or box, such as an ice cream tub for hatchlings, makes a good moist hide because they hold humidity well. Once you have the moist hide set up, all you need to do is ensure that the moss is kept damp by regularly spraying it and replacing it if and when it gets soiled. Not all keepers use moist hides for their retics and of those that do some keepers only provide a moist hide when the snake goes into a shed cycle, while others provide a box all the time that gives the snake the option to use it if they want.

Blocking ventilation – many vivariums come with vents set into the back, so if you are finding that your enclosure does not retain humidity well blocking some of these vents will help. However, remember to keep some ventilation to maintain airflow into and out of the vivarium.

Substrate

This is the material that lines the bottom of the enclosure. It is important to equip your set-up with some substrate to allow easier cleaning and protect the bottom of the enclosure.

Given that retics have a high frequency and volume of waste, regular cleaning is crucial to prevent ill health in your snake and to stop your house from smelling unpleasant. For many snakes it is sufficient to 'spot clean' enclosures and do a full clean out every few months. Spot cleaning is where you simply remove the fouled area and the substrate around it, while a full clean out would mean replacing all substrate and cleaning the enclosure. While spot cleaning can work well for retics, they will usually need fully cleaning out every few weeks due to the quantity and frequency of mess, especially urine as this

▲ Hatchling Pied Tiger retic on paper which makes a very practical substrate. Picture credit: Zack Thompson of Silver Spur Pythons

▲ An adult Lavender albino retic. Picture credit: Adam Walton

can be difficult to spot clean completely. It is often more practical to do a full clean out to ensure all of the mess is removed.

While there are other available substrates, this chapter will focus on the most popular that are used by retic keepers. If you are planning to use other substrates it is recommended that you do some of your own research to ensure that it is suitable for your snake. Some commonly used substrates are:

Paper – among the cheapest, most practical and hygienic of substrates is paper – such as newspaper, kitchen paper or any paper that is readily available – some people buy rolls of unprinted newspaper. It is cheap and very easy to use as a substrate, and it makes it very easy to spot any mess and fully clean out the enclosure each time. Another advantage of it compared to bark or similar substrates is that paper prevents bits of substrate getting stuck to the food items and being consumed during feeding. Paper is the preferred substrate for many retic keepers because it is easy to clean and maintain hygiene. The only downsides are that is it not very aesthetically pleasing and it doesn't hold humidity as well as some other substrates.

Aspen, bark chips and Lignocel *(a wood-based product that is soft and absorbent)* – These are similar in terms of their properties as a substrate. The main advantage over paper is their ability to hold humidity and that they are considered more visually attractive. If you use these substrates, a daily spray of water should ensure that the enclosure maintains good levels of humidity. The main disadvantages compared to paper are that it is more difficult to spot mess, it is more expensive – it will generally foul fairly rapidly and require regular replacement – and the possibility that it can get ingested by the snake during feeding. While rare, this has been linked with impaction – a digestive issue caused by ingesting something that cannot be easily digested or passed. Pieces of substrate can also get caught in the snake's mouth or teeth, which can cause irritation and infection.

AstroTurf or other synthetic fibres sold as reptile carpet – These can be used as a substrate, although this is less common than paper or bark chips. AstroTurf can also hold humidity well and be sprayed regularly, and it cannot be consumed like bark chips. However, it will need regular cleaning and/or replacing, which may make it too expensive and time consuming to maintain.

Plastic or lino flooring – preferably a type that is fully waterproof – can be practical at protecting the bottom of the enclosure, but is not absorbent and will not help to keep any mess away from the snake. This may be a very useful method for protecting the bottom of a wooden vivarium when used in combination with another form of substrate that can be easily cleaned out.

Bioactive set-ups – These are gaining popularity with reptile keepers and use natural methods to self-clean, which includes soil, bacteria and invertebrates that all feed upon the waste produced by a snake. These are more frequently used for smaller species of reptiles than retics, and this is likely to be due to the size of the enclosure and volume of substrate that is required to maintain a suitable level of bioactivity. This book doesn't provide further information on bioactive set-ups, but it may be something that you wish to consider and can research for yourself.

Substrate	Pros	Cons
Paper	Cheap, easy to spot mess, easy to clean, no risk of bits of substrate sticking to food.	Not aesthetically pleasing, not good at holding humidity.
Aspen, bark chips, Lignocel and similar	Able to hold humidity, aesthetically more pleasing than paper.	More difficult to spot and clean mess, expensive compared to paper, potential for bits to be consumed with food.
AstroTurf, reptile carpet and other synthetic fibres	Fully water proof, can be washed.	Can be time consuming to keep clean and expensive to replace.

Decoration (decor)

Retics, like most snakes, want to feel secure and despite being relatively active they will spend most of their time coiled up and not moving. Some keepers provide a lot of decor for their retics – partly for the snake's benefit and partly to make the set-up look more attractive. While other keepers, especially of adult snakes, use minimal decor.

For hatchlings, providing at least two hides – one at the hot end and one at the cold end of the enclosure – is very easy and will help your retic to feel secure. Hides can be made of almost anything, and there are a number that are marketed at reptile keepers. It is also possible (and cheaper) to make your own hides, for example out of large cardboard tubes, plastic drainpipes or flower pots or seed trays, among hundreds of other things that can also do the job.

For larger and adult retics, many keepers do not provide hides deciding that the enclosure forms a small and secure enough space for the snake to act as a suitable hide. Other keepers insist that hides are important to prevent the snake from displaying defensive behaviour such as hissing or striking. Large hides can be made from upturned dog beds or similar sized boxes, although cardboard boxes are unlikely to last long in

◄ *Hatchling retic using a hide.*

▼ *An upside-down cat litter tray or dog bed can make a good hide for larger retics.*

▲ *Albino retic in a well decorated naturalistic set-up. Picture credit: David van Berlo*

a humid enclosure with a large retic moving around. Individual snakes will differ as to whether they use the hides, but it is better to provide them and your snake does not use them, rather than not provide them and have a snake that doesn't feel secure.

Other decor that you may wish to consider for your set-up includes branches for climbing and fake plants and greenery. Real plants are not recommended, as they will get destroyed. Whatever you choose to include or not, you should consider whether it will:

- Help your snake feel secure and less exposed or vulnerable.
- Make it look visually appealing to you if so desired.
- Be securely fixed into the enclosure or movable without causing damage to the snake or the enclosure i.e. it is not ideal to stand a tree stump in the vivarium if your snake could knock it over and hurt itself.
- Be replaceable when trashed because only the most robust of decor will survive in an enclosure with a retic. Given the large amount of mess and the activity levels of a large-bodied snake, most decor ends up damaged over time.

▶ *A Really Useful Box (RUB) can be used as a large water bowl.*

Water bowl

A water bowl is a crucial part of your retic's set-up and your snake should never be kept in an enclosure without access to fresh water. Some keepers say that their retics like to soak in water, and in the wild they can often be found submerged in streams or ponds. As such, it is worth providing a water bowl that your snake can fully submerge in as well as drink from, should it choose to do so. In addition a large bowl will aid with maintaining humidity levels within the enclosure as the water evaporates.

Other keepers will claim that retics do not soak unless there is something wrong with them, for example the set-up might be too warm or too dry. Based on this, some prefer to offer a relatively small water bowl that the retic can drink from, but would not be able to fully submerge in. The truth is likely to be that every snake is an individual animal and some retics prefer soaking more than others, and that if conditions in the enclosure are not optimal the snake will be more likely to soak.

It is really important to keep the water clean, as water in warm areas – such as the inside of a retic enclosure – is a good place for bacteria to build up and breed, especially if urine or faeces is added. The water should be changed daily or more frequently if it gets fouled.

AUTHOR RECOMMENDATION – SUBSTRATE AND DECOR

● Keep your retics on paper or newspaper, as it is the most practical substrate and it will help you stay on top of cleaning and provide the most hygienic conditions for your snake.

● Use limited decor, such as suitably sized hides and large braches that are secured in the enclosure, as most other types will get trashed.

● Provide a large water bowl that the snake can submerge in.

● If you are unable to maintain sufficient levels of humidity, use a moist hide.

Lighting

In the wild, retics and many other snake species will actively bask in the sunlight, which not only helps with thermoregulation but also provides ultraviolet (UV) light, which is absorbed by the snake to help with vitamin D and calcium synthesis. Sunlight forms part of the natural day and night cycle for animals in the wild, which helps with natural behaviour such as basking.

In captivity, retics do not require light or UV to survive and breed healthily, but there is increasing evidence that providing it during the day can improve health and the condition of snakes including retics. There is little research to suggest whether it affects the growth of a retic or the longevity of its life.

Some keepers choose not to provide additional light – UV or otherwise – other than the natural room light. Should you wish to provide additional light this can be achieved by an LED strip or incandescent bulb(s) on a timer, which should be on for 11–12 hours a day. Ensure that any wires or fittings are suitably secure and guarded so the snake cannot damage the light or hurt itself. If the bulb produces additional heat you should make sure this doesn't alter the temperatures in the enclosure. This will help you to view your

▼ *Installing LED lights in your retic's enclosure can help view your snake and make the set-up look good. Picture credit: Darren Elson.*

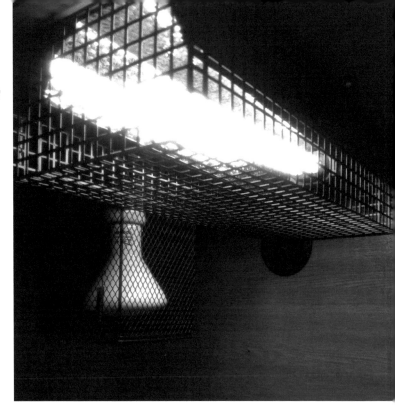

► *This photo shows the 24W ultraviolet (UV) light used in Envy's vivarium.*

retic and also to provide them with a natural day and night cycle similar to that found in Southeast Asia.

Using a light source that also emits UV light will provide the day and night cycle and will also provide the UV that the snake can use for vitamin D synthesis. The provision of UV will depend on the size of the enclosure – a small enclosure with little height for a baby retic will require low intensity and low wattage UV source, while a large enclosure will require higher wattage. You should research or seek specialist advice to determine the optimal level of UV to provide. For any light source used, ensure that any wires and fittings are suitably guarded and secure to prevent the snake from injuring itself or breaking the set-up.

AUTHOR RECOMMENDATION – LIGHTING

● Include UV in your set-up. Research the most suitable wattage and intensity for your enclosure's size, and make sure you change the bulb as recommended by the manufacturer.

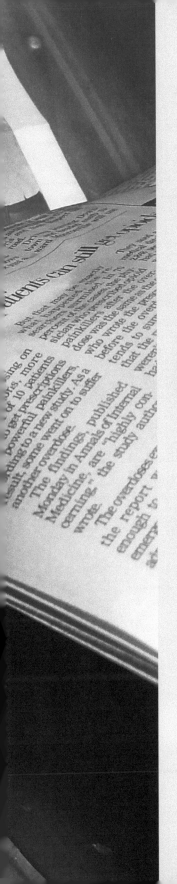

CHAPTER 4

MAINTENANCE

Picture credit: Rob Rausch

Cleaning, feeding and shedding

The maintenance for keeping a retic is relatively straightforward. You will have to provide food and water, ensure that the enclosure is kept clean and that it is maintained correctly, including temperatures and humidity.

Cleaning

Cleaning up is one of the less glamorous parts of owning a retic. When you have a large snake that is eating large items of food, you have to clean up a large mess. Retics have relatively fast metabolisms compared to many snake species and they also tend to drink a lot of water.

When the snake has urinated or defecated the mess should be cleaned up as soon as possible. It is often most practical to move the snake to a holding enclosure or plastic box while cleaning. If your snake is being kept on paper then a full clean out is straightforward, while on substrate such as bark chips it may be possible to 'spot clean' i.e. remove only the soiled area and the area of substrate around the mess. However, with retics the quantity and frequency of mess may mean that even with bark chips or similar substrate, spot cleaning may not be sufficient. Instead, a full clean is needed regularly as the substrate will become saturated with urine.

The enclosure can be cleaned with warm water or by using steam. Avoid chemicals that are not safe for animals or those that leave a strong smell. There are a number of different veterinary disinfectants such as F10 that are suitable for use when cleaning a snake enclosure.

Feeding

In the wild, retics eat a wide variety of prey items including mammals, birds and lizards. They are capable of eating very large items, some of which may be up to a quarter of the length of the snake and the same weight.

Retics are known for having a very strong feeding response and it is important to consider this and be aware of it when feeding the animal. A large proportion of accidental bites that occur are around feeding or when there is a smell of the snake's food around. In general these accidents can be avoided by being careful around feeding time and recognising that the snake will be expecting food. When handling snake food, do not handle your retic or any other snakes. When feeding the snake wearing gloves can mask the heat signature of your hand and help to prevent the snake mistaking your hand for

▶ *A Really Useful Box (RUB) being used to hold Envy while her enclosure is cleaned out.*

food. Equipment such as tongs and grabbers can be used to offer food to your retic while staying out of reach of the snake if it mistakes your hand for food. Some retics will take a food item that is left on the floor, while others prefer to take it from the tongs by striking and grabbing the food with their mouth and coiling around it as if the food were alive.

Retics in captivity will usually accept a range of whole prey items, including mice, rats, rabbits, chicks, quails, chickens, goat kids, piglets, lambs and others. It is important to find somewhere that can supply food sources for large retics as larger food items are less common than small ones in pet shops. In general rats for young snakes are ideal, and then as the snake gets bigger rabbits are the preferred choice of food for many keepers, making up the majority of a retic's diet. Some animals – for example Dwarfs and small males – may remain small enough that large rats are enough throughout their lives, and they do not require bigger items.

A lot of keepers vary their snake's diet with the occasional alternative food item. This can be important for young snakes to prevent them from getting used to one type of food and then not accepting alternatives later. An example of this is when trying to move from feeding rats to rabbits – a snake that has only ever eaten rats may not take to them. While a retic can survive on rats without this being detrimental to the snake's health, it will cost you more money buying multiple large rats for each feed rather than a single rabbit.

The size of the food item will depend on the size of the retic. Hatchlings will eat something the size of a large mouse, day-old chick or fuzzy (baby) rat/small weaner rat, while adults are commonly fed on rabbits, multiple XL rats and larger items if offered.

The size of the food items should be around 1.5 times the thickness of the widest part of the snake. Of course, this is approximate and it will be difficult to achieve this for each feed, especially if you are providing multiple items. In the wild, retics are opportunists

▼ *Feeding equipment including long tongs, a grabber and gloves should be used when feeding retics. Picture credit: Zack Thompson of Silver Spur Pythons*

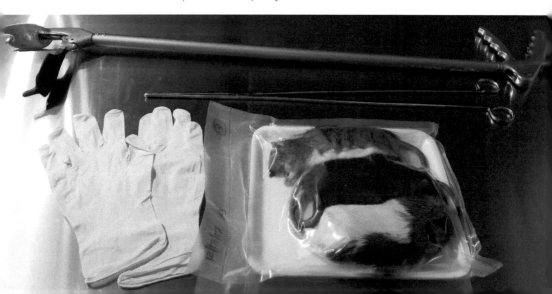

▲ *A young retic being offered a small rat from long tongs. Picture credit. Zack Thompson of Silver Spur Pythons*

▶ *Young Albino Golden Child eating a small rat. Picture credit: Zack Thompson of Silver Spur Pythons*

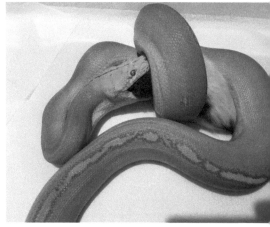

and will eat small food items or things that are far larger than this if given the chance. The frequency of the feeding will also depend on the age of the retic and size of the prey item relative to the snake.

In the wild, retics will not eat at regular intervals – they will sometimes get meals close together and other times have to wait for long periods of time. As such, in captivity they will often accept food items offered after short intervals. This is generally not an issue for young retics who will eat frequently and grow rapidly. However, it can cause issues if this is continued over a prolonged period of time and can lead to obesity, particularly for adult snakes or for those approaching adulthood as their growth rate slows.

Retics, as with many snakes in captivity, are prone to obesity and obesity-related issues, which can cause strain on internal organs and might shorten the snake's life. If it appears that your retic is gaining excess weight, you may wish to adjust the feeding routine, either by missing a feed, generally lengthening the time between feeds or offering smaller meals.

Likewise, if your retic looks like it is becoming underweight, which may be apparent if the backbone is particularly visible under the skin, then you may wish to increase the food size or frequency. If the retic rapidly becomes underweight then you should take it to the vet to rule out any underlying causes – they can go for long periods of time without food, but do not usually lose weight quickly, so rapid weight loss may be a sign of something seriously wrong. Generally it is easier to overfeed a retic than underfeed it.

Young retics have been known to suffer from constipation or impaction – this means it is important to monitor that your snake is defecating regularly. They will often do so several days after eating a meal – again, this can be shorter for hatchlings and longer for adults. In general try not to feed your retic if it hasn't defecated since its last meal. While it is unlikely that it will cause any issues if it happens occasionally, if it occurs repeatedly your snake may become constipated, which can lead to a rectal prolapse. This is where rectal tissue is pushed out of the snake's body often through the act of defecation. If this happens, move the snake onto damp paper substrate to prevent the tissue from drying out while keeping it clean and take the animal to a vet as soon as possible.

If your retic hasn't defecated in a while, a common solution is to give the snake a bath for about 20 minutes in warm water – around 27°C (80°F) – and this may help to resolve the issue. This can be done in a small plastic tub or a bath, depending on the size of retic – just add enough water to cover the snake's body while it is in it.

Some retics will not eat during the period before they shed their skins. Most keepers tend not to feed while they are preparing to shed, which is a good idea as it lets the snake's

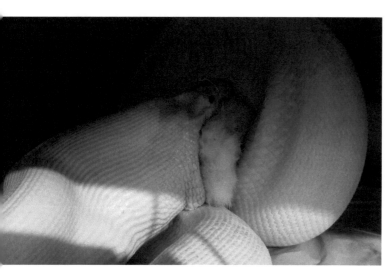

◀ *Adult Ivory retic eating a rabbit. Picture credit: Zack Thompson of Silver Spur Pythons*

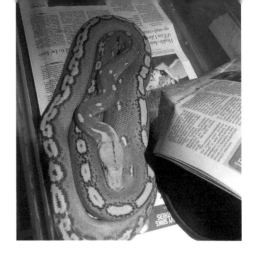

▶ *A young retic after eating, showing the food bulge that will be digested over the next couple of days. Picture credit: Rob Rausch*

body and digestive system rest. Some snakes will continue to accept food while in shed – retics are one of the species more likely to continue to eat – but it will depend on the individual snake. Having said this, eating while in shed will not cause any health issues for your retic although it is possible that it can lead to a worse shed and stuck skin. If you do leave it to shed without food, most retics will keenly accept it again once the shed is complete.

Here is a suggested feeding schedule that may be useful as a starting point, although it will need to be adjusted for your individual circumstances for feeding appropriately sized meals:

- Hatchlings, every five to seven days.
- Six to 12 months old, every seven to 10 days.
- 12–24 months old, every 10–14 days.
- 24+ months old, every two to three weeks.

This is very rough guide and should be adjusted for the individual snake's needs and based on its growth. Keeping a record of when your snake has eaten and shed its skin will help you to monitor its development.

AUTHOR RECOMMENDATION – FEEDING

- Provide a diet predominantly of rats or rabbits with occasional variation such as chickens or lambs.

- Follow a rough feeding schedule as outlined above.

- In general, avoid feeding while the snake is in shed.

◄ *Envy showing some retained shed before she was soaked in warm water to gently remove the skin. Picture credit: Natasha James*

Shedding

Retics, like all snakes, shed their skin regularly. This involves the very top layer of each scale (including over the eye) lifting off and being shed. It generally happens every four to six weeks depending on age and growth – generally more frequently for young snakes and less frequently for adults. Around a week to 10 days before shedding the snake will go into 'blue' as it prepares to shed. The top layer of scales start to lift off and a thin layer of oil gets between the layers to help when the snake actually sheds. This period is often characterised by a dulling of the snake's colours and a grey/blue sheen over the eyes, hence the term going into 'blue.'

Snakes generally become less active during this time and may become less willing to be handled. This can involve displaying defensive behaviour like shrugging their bodies and huffing, since this is a time when the snake will feel more vulnerable – possibly due to their compromised sight during this time. The snake may also prefer the cool end of the vivarium or a moist hide if one has been provided.

In retics, going into blue is sometimes accompanied by a slight red/pink tinge to the belly scales – this can look like the very early stages of scale rot. It is also reported by some keepers that when in blue a retic's breathing can become louder with a slight but audible 'hiss/huff' to each exhalation – this can sound like the very early stages of a respiratory infection. As such, it is important to know your retic and their usual behaviour – including their shed cycles – so that you can monitor these signs.

When your retic is in blue before a shed, it becomes more important to maintain or increase humidity, since dry skin becomes more difficult to shed and may become stuck to the snake. To help it, a daily spraying of the enclosure will add additional humidity if needed.

If the snake doesn't shed fully and there is some stuck skin this can cause an irritation to the animal. Over time a build-up of stuck shed can lead to sores and infections. Shed is most likely to get stuck around the eyes or head, the tip of the tail or the cloaca or vent area. The best way to help to remove stuck shed is to give the snake a soak – either in a bath or a warm damp pillow case, which will make the skin easier to remove. You can then help by gently picking pieces off or running the snake through a damp towel until all the skin is removed.

▼ *Retics will often soak as they prepare to shed. Picture credit: Matthew Genser*

Handling and tap training

Handling retics can be one of the most rewarding parts about keeping them, although you are likely to need a lot of time and effort. Retics used to have a reputation for being aggressive and difficult to handle, however this often stems back to early animals in captivity when many were caught in the wild and had not adjusted to being kept in captivity with regular interaction with humans. The majority of retics kept in Europe and the US are now captive bred and many of these are very even-tempered and reluctant to bite. They become accustomed to being handled regularly, although hatchlings can be a little snappy.

It can be difficult or intimidating to get a retic from its enclosure since it can be nervous or react as if being fed. With regular calm handling, perhaps building up to four or five times a week over many years, you will be able to build a trusting bond with your retic and have a very rewarding snake to handle, especially when this is done from a hatchling.

Retics are very active and inquisitive snakes and will explore their surroundings when out of the enclosure. They are also reasonably good climbers – much more so than other large pythons. When handling a retic it is important to support as much of its weight as possible, as is the case for most snakes. Try not to grab the animal, and instead gently let it move through your hands while you support from underneath. Many retics will be not be tolerant of their head or tail – the relatively short section after the cloaca – being

▼ *With regular interaction retics can become very accustomed to being handled. Picture credit: Ed Taoka*

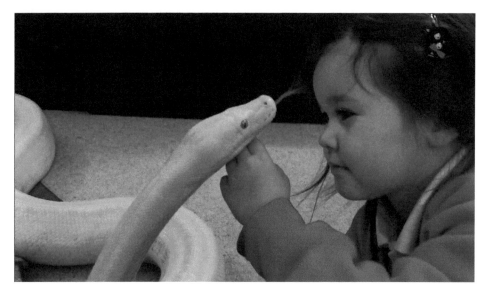

▶ *Handling retics can be a rewarding part of keeping these animals. Picture credit: Krystle Anderson and Zack Thompson*

▼ *Once out of their enclosure, the majority of retics will be calm and explore their surroundings or find somewhere to sit and get comfortable. Picture credit: Natasha James*

touched or grabbed, but in most cases the snake will simply take avoiding action rather than becoming aggressive.

It is important to try to avoid handling your snake for 24–48 hours after feeding and while the snake is in 'blue', where possible to avoid stressing your snake.

Retics, like other large snake – and indeed many large animals – can be dangerous and cause severe injuries if they feel threatened or in danger. They can cause a lot of damage with their bite – they have a row of teeth that point backwards and are sharp on the back – which males use for fighting with other males. If you get bitten as a feeding response, which may lead to the snake holding on, spraying vinegar in the retics mouth or running the snake under cold water should make it let go. As such, it can be useful to keep a bit of neat vinegar in a small spray bottle near the enclosure.

For your own safety and the safety of your retic you should always be careful when handling your animal. Ensure that you have at least one other person present when handling it. It is commonly advised that you have at least one person for every 1.8m (6ft) of snake – i.e. for snakes up to 1.8m (6ft) you have one person, for snakes 1.8–3.6m (6–12ft) you have two people, and so on.

While many retics are very calm and will not cause a problem when being handled, you should always keep in mind that these are very powerful creatures and should you get bitten they can cause a lot of damage. For the benefit of all snake keepers, it is important to understand that these animals receive negative attention in the media and that can be detrimental to public opinion for those of us that love retics. **So please be responsible when handling and interacting with these snakes**.

Tap training is a simple technique often used for handling large-bodied snakes, although it can be used on any species. Retics seem to be very responsive to this technique and it is widely used by keepers due to their feeding response. While it is called tap training, it is more of a conditioning technique rather than actually training the snake. The idea behind it is that when you open the enclosure, rather than reach straight in you 'tap' i.e. gently stroke the snake on the head or neck with a stick or snake hook. After this 'tap' you can then reach in and gently pick up the snake.

Over time the animal will learn to associate the 'tap' with being picked up and that it is not associated with feeding. As you observe your snake's behaviour you will learn to recognise when it is responding to the tap training. While the primary aim is to 'turn off' the feeding response, it also seems to serve a secondary purpose in that it lets the snake know that it is about to be picked up, which avoids surprising the animal and leads to less defensive behaviour.

If you are going to use tap training, it is recommended that you start while the snake is a hatchling or still young. However, if that is not possible then it is still beneficial to start tap training as soon as you start handling your retic, although you may have to be aware that it could take a little time for the snake to get used to it.

During breeding season – September to December – mature males can become difficult to handle. In the wild they would be searching for females at this time and so will be much more active in their enclosure. They will also be aggressive towards other males, and will possibly fight and cause fatal injuries. A male retic during breeding season

▶ *Many keepers use snake hooks for tap training their retics or for assisting with handling difficult snakes.*

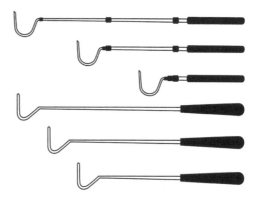

◄ *Male motley golden child during a breeding season, showing interest in breeding by arching his body. Picture credit: Scott Cochrane of SC Pythons*

will often arch his body against the side of the enclosure. During this time it is especially important to be careful when handling male retics, as they will often be a lot more active and less tolerant to being picked up. If you have other retics being kept nearby you should try to ensure you do not carry the scent of other males on your clothes or hands when handling one. It may also be worth moving adult female retics away from males, which may help to calm their behaviour.

Some retics will push on their enclosures with their nose, which can be distressing for an owner to observe and can cause damage to the scales on the snake's head. This may lead to an open wound and infection, or could cause damage to the teeth. Males especially may push during the breeding season, but this behaviour is not restricted to males or limited to the breeding season. One way to reduce this behaviour is to cover the front of the enclosure with a sheet so that they cannot see out – this seems to work relatively well for males during breeding season. Another thing to try is to increase the feeding slightly by offering larger food or feeding more frequently – this seems to help for females that are pushing, especially young females that are still growing.

AUTHOR RECOMMENDATION – HANDLING

- Regular calm handling will generally lead to a snake that is tolerant of it.

- Use tap training from a young age if possible.

- Don't handle after feeding or when the snake is in shed.

CHAPTER 5

GENETIC MORPHS

Picture credit: Robert Euvino

What is a Genetic Morph?

With captive bred retics and many other snakes, it is often desirable to breed them to produce offspring with colour or pattern changes compared to their natural or wild appearance. These alternate colours or patterns are often caused by a genetic mutation, which can be passed down to the snake's offspring. Due to the popularity of these mutations they are often considered as favourable and are referred to as morphs.

An example of such a morph is albino, where the snake lacks colour pigment in the scales due to the absence of melanin. While it is rare, albino snakes do occur naturally in the wild, where it is not a favourable mutation since albino snakes are more likely to be spotted by predators. However, in captivity the albino colouring in many species of snakes is popular with keepers and they are selectively bred in large numbers. Throughout this chapter these favourable genetic mutations will be referred to as genetic morphs.

How do these Morphs occur?

Genetic morphs in retics and other snakes usually occur via a small number of animals that exhibit the aberrant colour or pattern in question, and these individuals are then selectively bred to determine whether the colour or pattern is genetic by seeing whether it passes on to future generations. A lot of the morphs that are available in captive bred retics have come from single specimens that showed a genetic difference from others. These mutations in the original snakes are likely to be due to spontaneous mutation, where something altered the genetic sequence for that individual snake, which can then be passed to its offspring.

Since morphs express themselves genetically they are often referred to as being different genes. In some case this may be inaccurate since it is possible that different morphs may be a different allele of the same gene rather than different genes, i.e. a variant form of the same gene. Different alleles can produce different phenotypes, i.e. the observable characteristics of an organism. For example the gene for eye colour has different alleles that create different phenotypes, e.g. blue or brown eyes.

As with other snakes, multiple genetic morphs can be bred into a single retic. Unlike some snake species, these combinations tend to be described by the list of individual morphs that they have rather than being referred to by a new name, although there are some exceptions. For example, the combination of Tiger Anthrax is referred to as Clown.

Due to this, the number of possible combinations is huge and this book cannot list all available permutations. Instead, this chapter will list the most commonly available single gene morphs that are available at the time of writing, but bear in mind that new morphs are found all the time and new combinations are bred each year. There are a lot of online resources and reptile keeping groups that can provide information on new multiple gene combinations.

Genetic morphs can be passed on to the snake's offspring because genes come in pairs, and so in each snake there are two copies of each gene – one that came from the mother's DNA and one from the father's. If a snake inherits only one copy of a gene from either parent, that snake is referred to as being heterozygous (het for short) for that gene. If a snake inherits a copy of the same gene from each parent then the snake is said to be homozygous for that gene.

As mentioned above, a snake can inherit multiple morphs. In the case where the snake inherits a single copy of two different genes the snake would usually be describe as a double heterozygous, which may be written as DH.

▼ *Multi-gene retic – Platinum Motley Supertiger. Picture credit: Clayton Arnott*

However, it is possible for a snake to inherit two different morphs that are allelic, i.e. at the same part of the gene so that a chromosomal pair is made up of one copy of each allelic morph. This is referred to as being compound heterozygous, and is slightly different to DH, since DH will have a single copy of two morphs that are on different chromosomal pairs. This is covered in more detail when discussing albino colouring.

If we know what type of gene or allele led to the morph and whether the snake is heterozygous or homozygous, we can understand how the offspring will carry the gene and whether the morph will be expressed visually. Below are listed different types of genetic traits and how they interact from parent to offspring.

Types of Genetic Morph

Recessive

For genetic traits that are recessive the snake needs to inherit two copies of the gene for the genetic trait to be expressed so that we see the change in colour or pattern from the wild type. That means the snake needs to have a copy of the gene from each parent, i.e. to be homozygous for the gene.

If a snake inherits a copy of a recessive gene from only one parent, i.e. be heterozygous for the gene, the gene will not be expressed visually and the snake will show the wild-type retic colour and pattern. Compound heterozygous is the slight exception to this in that being compound het may lead to altered colour and/or pattern. A heterozygous snake will still be able to pass the gene onto their offspring – approximately half of the offspring will receive a copy of the gene from a heterozygous parent. Both parents need to carry at least one copy of the gene for a recessive gene to be visually expressed by the offspring.

◄ Fury's colours show why the albino gene is a very popular recessive gene in retics. Picture credit: Natasha James

▶ *Tiger is a very popular incomplete dominant gene, with the homozygous form being referred to as Supertiger. This photo shows Envy's Tiger patterning when she was a yearling. Credit: Natasha James*

Pairing a heterozygous snake with one that is either heterozygous or homozygous for the same recessive gene will mean there is a chance that some of the offspring will express the gene, i.e. be homozygous for the gene and will have the visual appearance of the morph in question.

One of the most common examples of a recessive gene is albino, so for a snake to visually show the albino gene and the lack of colour pigment, it needs to inherit a copy of the albino gene from both the mother and father. A retic that is heterozygous for albino will show the wild-type colour and pattern.

Incomplete dominance

For genetic traits in snakes incomplete dominance is often referred to as co-dominance, which can be confusing because the two are slightly different – co-dominance is described below. The majority of retic morphs that may be described as co-dominant are in fact incomplete dominant.

Incomplete dominant genes can be considered in the same way as for recessive, but the heterozygous form is visually different from retics that do not carry the gene. As such the heterozygous form is often given a name of its own. The homozygous form – where the snake carries two copies of the gene – is visually different from retics that carry no copies of the gene and from retics that carry one copy. The homozygous form is often called the Super form – for example, Tiger is the incomplete dominant gene for Supertiger.

Dominant traits

If a genetic trait is dominant the offspring only needs to receive one copy of the gene from the parents for the trait to be visually expressed. In reticulated pythons many genes that were thought to be dominant are actually incomplete dominant, for example Tiger was thought to be dominant until the homozygous form – Supertiger – was produced. While Tiger does behave like a dominant gene in the sense that the offspring only needs to receive one copy of the gene to be a visual Tiger, the difference is that if the snake receives two copies then the snake will be a Supertiger. As such Tiger could be considered as the visual heterozygous form of the gene Supertiger.

Co-dominance

This is where a recessive and a dominant trait appear together to produce a third combination. As an example, imagine you have a flower with a dominant red gene and crossed it with a flower with a recessive white gene. If the genes were incomplete-dominant you may get a pink flower, while if the genes were co-dominant you may get a red flower with white stripes. There are no genes that are currently thought to be co-dominant with the natural or wild-type appearance of retics.

Common Genetic Morphs in Reticulated Pythons

It is useful to note that many morphs and even retics with wild-type colours go through some colour change as they grow from hatchling to adult, as well as some daily colour change in terms of being darker or lighter. When deciding whether you want a morph and which type, it may be useful to see adults as well as hatchlings so that you can get an idea of the possible appearance of an adult if you are buying a hatchling. This colour change as they mature is called 'onto-genetic.'

Where possible, this book tries to include information about the origin of each of the morphs covered below. It is almost impossible to know the exact origin for each morph, so where relevant the book states breeders that have been known to work with the gene, although this is not to say they are the only people to have done so.

Recessive Morphs

Albino

The general appearance of Albino in retics and other animals is characterised by the complete or partial absence of the dark pigment melanin in the skin. Albino retics show beautiful white, yellow, orange, purple and grey tones. The albino gene does not alter the normal patterning of retics in general, although it can lead to elongated pattern when combined with other genes.

There are many different phenotypes or strains of albino in retics. Many of these are listed below. It appears that these are all different expressions, or alleles, of a single gene. The appearance of difference strains of albino can vary considerable in terms of the levels of purple, orange and yellow colours in particular, but are all characterised by the absence or partial absence of dark pigment and colouration.

▶ A close-up of Fury showing that the albino gene retains the wild-type patterning while removing the dark pigment from the colours. Picture credit: Natasha James

Some strains of albino are compatible with other strains and the influence from two strains of albino can be present in an individual retic. The combinations of different albino strains are thought to be compound heterozygous, i.e. they have a single copy of the alleles for the two albino strains, which occur at the same locus of the gene. This differs from being double heterozygous for different recessive genes because a snake that is compound heterozygous will be visually different from a wild-type retic, while a double het for different recessive genes would not alter the wild-type appearance. Also, a double het retic would be able to pass on both of the genes for which it was het. While for compound hets, since the alleles are on the same part of the gene the retic will pass on one of the albino strains to its offspring, but cannot pass on both. Examples are provided below for individual strains.

Type I Clark Albino – White and purple albino
(compound het: Lavender)

In April 1994 Bob Clark obtained a retic that was caught in Myanmar from a dealer in Malaysia after photos showed that the snake was yellow, white and faded purple in colour and lacking black pigment. This indicated it was an albino, although it was slightly different to other albino pythons in captivity at the time, i.e. Royal pythons and Burmese pythons, which were mostly yellow and white in colour.

The first captive born Clark strain albinos were hatched in 1999. The offspring varied in colour – all of the albinos showing oranges and yellows, but the background colour varied between white, faded purple and darker purple. At the time this led to Clark albinos being divided into three sub-strains – White, Lavender and Purple.

It was later determined that the original male was a compound heterozygous for two separate compatible strains of albino – White and Purple. The compound heterozygous form is also visually albino since the White and Purple phenotypes occur on the same part of the gene, and this form was named Lavender albino. Lavender retics show a faded purple or lavender colour rather than the purple or white of the two strains. A Lavender retic can pass on a gene for either White or Purple albino to its offspring, but cannot pass on both. To make visually albino hatchlings a Lavender retic would need to be bred with another retic that had at least one copy of a compatible albino gene (either heterozygous or homozygous).

◄ *Albino retics are very popular and the albino gene is often combined with many other genes, meaning there are a huge range of albino combinations available. Picture credit: Matthew Judge*

▼ *An adult White albino retic. Picture credit: Liam Saville*

▼ *A Purple albino retic. Picture credit: Weston Wenner*

▼ *An adult Lavender albino retic. Picture credit: Karl Emery*

▲ *Foulsham Caramel hatchlings from the same clutch. Picture credit: Karl Emery*

Foulsham Caramel

The original Foulsham Caramel was owned by Peter Foulsham in the UK who established that it was a separate line from other retics that were thought to be Caramels at the time. Foulsham Caramels have rich cream and orange colours and the purples are quite dark, almost grey. Foulsham Caramel is compatible with Clark Purple and White and the compound heterozygotes are called Amaretto (Foulsham and Purple) and Coral (Foulsham and White).

Indo Caramel

Indo Caramel retics have been imported to the US from a breeding facility in Indonesia. The original female Indo Caramel retic in the US was hatched in 2008. While it was thought to be Indo Caramel it was later proven to be an Orangeglow (OG), which is the compound het for Indo Caramel and Clark albino. The original female was Orangeglow het Clark White albino.

Some of the first actual Indo Caramels that were produced in the US were in 2015 by:
● Robert Euvino in an unlikely fashion through a pairing that should not have yielded Indo Caramels. This single Indo Caramel came from a pairing between a Lemonglow het Indo Caramel male and a Leucistic female (Leucistic from unknown origin, but most likely Lemonglow).

• Michael Derr with the first clutch intended to produce Indo Caramels from a Motley Tiger Orangeglow male and an Orangeglow female.

• Tyree Jimerson and Greg Vicoli who also produced Indo Caramels from a pairing between a 2010 Orangeglow male and a 2009 Sunfire het Indo Caramel female.

Quite a few other Indo Caramels and Orangeglows have been imported from Indonesia since the original Orangeglow was imported. Of these, nearly all of them have proved to be Orangeglows.

Indo Caramel retics are very dark albinos with very little white and the usual black replaced with strong brown and gold colours. The sides are bright orange and yellow and the underside is cream or white. The Indo Caramel gene is compatible with Clark White and Purple Albino producing the compound heterozygous Orangeglow. There is very little difference between het White and het Purple Orangeglows, so without knowing the parents it is unreliable to determine this based on appearance, hence both are referred to as Orangeglow.

▼ *Indo Caramel retic. Picture credit: Tyree Jimerson*

Mocha

One of the first Mochas in the US was a WC male obtained by Salvador Veleta in around 2010, who also named the gene. It may be that there are several lines in the US and Europe that are slightly different. As with Indo Caramel these retics are relatively dark albinos, the black pattern is replaced with dark gold and the colours along the back and sides can vary from light brown to cream with bright yellow and orange along the sides. Mocha is also compatible with White and Purple Albino, producing a combination called Mochino – which is the compound het for Mocha and either Clark White or Purple.

Table of compond heterozygotes for different starins of albino in reticulated pythons

Albino Strains	Clark White	Clark Purple	Indo Caramel	Mocha	Foulsham Caramel
Clark White	—	Lavender	Orangeglow het White	Mochino het White	Coral
Clark Purple	Lavender	—	Orangeglow het Purple	Mochino het Purple	Amaretto
Indo Caramel	Orangeglow het White	Orangeglow het Purple	—	Mochino het Mocha	?*
Mocha	Mochino het White	Mochino het Purple	Indo Caramel Mocha	—	Foulsham Caramel Mocha
Foulsham Caramel	Coral	Amaretto	?*	Foulsham Caramel Mocha	—

* It is thought that Indo and Foulsham Caramel would be compatible, but this is currently unconfirmed

Type II Albino

Type II albinos, also known as Amels (Amelanistic), are another strain of albino that differs from the Clark Purple or White albino. Type II also originally came from a wild-caught retic from Malaysia that Bob Clark acquired. This albino is characterised by bright lemon yellows. Type II albino is compatible with Blonde albino.

Blonde Albino

A third form of albino, which Bob Clark referred to as Blonde, originated in a wild-caught pair of albinos that were imported from Malaysia. Blonde albinos are characterised by being much less white and having deeper yellows and oranges than other albinos. It is compatible with Type II Amel albino.

Blonde albino hatchlings are very light in colour, similar to Type II Amel albinos and as they grow they darken into very dark albinos with high levels of gold, yellow and purple.

▲ *Adult Type II albino (Amel). Picture credit: Zack Thompson of Silver Spur Pythons*

▶ *A young adult Blonde albino. Picture credit: Zack Thompson of Silver Spur Pythons*

Renick Ghost Albino

Renick Ghost (albino) is another line of albino that was proven by Ben Renick in 2010. Renick Ghost has darker purple colours than a Clark Type I Purple albino, which are outlined in a yellow pinstripe while the rest of the snake remains a bone-white colour. The original male was imported from Indonesia but it is not known where the snake was captured. In recent years more males of similar genetics have been found in Northern Sumatra around Medan City, which is the only known place where this gene has been found. Renick Ghost is not compatible with Clark White and Purple or Type II albino, which suggests it will not work with other strains including Mocha, Indo Caramel or Blonde.

◄ *The original wild-caught Renick Ghost male, owned by Ben Renick. Picture credit: Ben Renick, supplied by Travis Warren*

► *A close up of a Renick Ghost Genetic Stripe. Picture credit: Travis Warren*

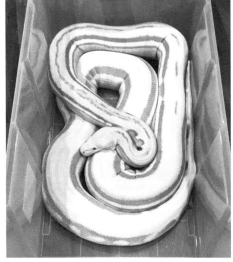

▲ A Renick Ghost Genetic Stripe. Picture credit: Travis Warren

◄ A Genetic Stripe retic. Picture credit: Travis Warren

Type III Albino

There is a Type III albino that has also been bred by Bob Clark. It is similar to White albino but is not compatible with Clark White and Purple or Type II albino, and relatively small numbers have been bred.

Sharp Albino

This was originally imported and proved to be genetic by Brian Sharp. As with Type III albino, it is similar to White albino and also does not appear to be compatible with other strains of albino.

Honeyblast Albino

Honeyblast retics were first hatched in the UK to Imperial Retics. The original wild-caught male was obtained by Imperial Retics and appeared to be visually different to other albinos. It has been proven to be incompatible with Clark White and Purple albinos and with Foulsham Caramels, which proved Honeyblast to be a separate and new strain of albino. In April 2015 Imperial Retics hatched the first visual Honeyblast retics, which are almost identical to other amelanistic retics and darken as they mature, similar to Blondes.

Genetic Stripe

Genetic Stripe (GS) originated from a wild-caught female in Indonesia. The original female was owned by Bob Clark in 1996. There was also a male striped retic in the UK that was thought to have been imported from Indonesia at a similar time, which was also later acquired by Bob Clark. The original pair of GS retics grew to around 3.6–4.0m (12–13ft) in length, indicating that they originated from a smaller mid-sized locality. More recently photographs were found of a third wild-caught GS retic that was captured on Madura Island off the coast of East Java. It has been confirmed that several wild retics showing the same pattern as GS have been found on and around Madura and East Java.

GS retics show a striped pattern along the body rather than the typical wild-type reticulated pattern. The white rosettes on the side of GS retics are generally elongated to the point where they form a stripe all along the body. The black, silver and brown colours also form stripes along the length of the snake, which leads to a very clean looking animal with attractive contrast between the colours. The body colour below the side stripes ranges from a grey to a beautiful blue colour and the dorsal top colour ranges from silver to light tan.

Due to the original wild-caught GS being relatively small, GS was one of the earliest morphs that were considered as Dwarf.

Anerythristic/Anery

Anery retics are thought have first been bred by Prehistoric Pets in Fountain Valley, California, around 2007 and is one of the few morphs that is thought to have originated from a Super Dwarf retic.

This is a recessive gene that greatly reduces the red pigment from the base colours, which is the same as the Anery gene in other snakes. Anery retics retain the silver, black and yellow colouration and the typical reticulated pattern.

◀ *This Ultra Ivory Anery shows the effect that Anery has when compared to the Ultra Ivory gene below, in that this retic displays a reduction in the warm yellow, orange and red pigments. Picture credit: Matthew Genser*

▲ *An adult Titanium retic named Trevor. Picture credit: Joanna Aldwinckle*

Titanium

Titanium is first credited as being bred by Prehistoric Pets in California around 2006–07. The Titanium gene produces a wide variation in colour and pattern, with Titanium retics being generally brown, orange and gold snakes, often without pattern, although the Titanium gene can produce examples that vary from grey, silver or nearly black to snakes that are nearly yellow with some black along the back or sides.

The heterozygous form of Titanium is sometimes referred to as Citron since it can produce a subtle change to the wild-type appearance by increasing yellow colours, although this is often an unreliable way to tell whether a retic is het Titanium.

◀ A beautiful pair of twins – Pied hatchlings still in the egg. Picture credit: Heather Hodsdon and Dean Turner, the Reptile Room

▼ A Pied retic. Picture credit: Raul Garcia

Piebald (Pied)

Mike Wilbanks of Constrictors Unlimited in Oklahoma City acquired the original wild-caught male from Indonesia in the autumn of 2005 after seeing pictures of the snake and realising it was an important example in terms of retic genetics. After collecting the snake Mike compared the retic to a low white Pied Royal python. He described the retic by saying "The colour is a steel blue/grey and the pattern is completely replaced with black and gold speckles. The tongue is pale pink and the eyes are dark blue. The belly is completely pied white with patches extending up the sides." Bob Clark then acquired the snake in 2007 and bred it that year hoping that all the hatchlings were het for Pied. In 2011 the first eggs from one of the possible het Pied retics hatched, producing hatchlings resembling the Pied pattern of the original Pied retic although with varying degrees of white. There have since been several more reports of low white Pied retics that have been caught in Sumatra.

The Pied gene removes colour pigment from parts of the animal, leaving areas of white scales and areas of coloured pattern. Pied also alters the typical reticulated pattern so that the sections of the retic that are non-white are often left with mostly browns and greys, with little black and yellow. As with all Pied animals the pattern is variable between snakes – some show only a small amount of white, while others are almost completely white.

Anthrax

Anthrax retics were first produced by New England Reptile Distributors (NERD) who acquired a male Anthrax and bred him to a snake called Poison Ivy who was a Calico. Other retics with a similar appearance to Anthrax have been caught in Sumatra, making them one of the most common genes found in the wild.

Anthrax is characterised by a broken striped pattern of white along the top of the sides with highlights of yellow. There is generally more patterning and speckling along the back in browns and blacks than GS. Anthrax does not usually show grey or silver along the sides that are often present on GS.

Retics that are het Anthrax, sometime called Graniteback, can have patterns that range from almost normal in appearance to extremely irregular or broken along the whole body, and in some cases the black is reduced to speckling rather than solid patterning. However, it can be difficult to visually determine whether a retic is het for Anthrax so the name Graniteback is not always used.

▶ *A male Anthrax Tiger and one of his offspring. Picture credit: Heather Hodsdon and Dean Turner, the Reptile Room*

▲ *Orange Ghost Stripe Tiger. Picture credit: Scott Cochrane of SC Pythons*

Orange Ghost Stripe (OGS)

OGS retics are credited to have been first bred by New England Reptile Distributors (NERD) in 2008 and originated in a retic said to be a Dwarf from Selayar. Several more OGS have been found in the wild since then and all have been from East Java, which has made some people question whether the original OGS was from Selayar. OGS is compatible with Phantom that produces the morph referred to as Cow – a white snake that develops black spots as it grows.

OGS retics usually contain a dorsal stripe and a regular pattern of blotches or row of colour along their back. The rosettes are often clear and surrounded by a small amount of black outline or patterning. Hatchlings start out dark in colour, almost brown and brighten to gold and orange with age, often becoming very bright as adults.

Calico

This is an interesting gene that is very unpredictable in retics. It mostly affects the colour, but can also alter the pattern slightly often creating a patchwork effect where some parts show relatively normal colours while others show areas of low black, heavy whites, silvers or yellows. Calico has been observed in other animals, such as cats, where it is as equally unpredictable and not fully understood.

The majority of Calico retics are caught in the wild. There are many different strains that are labelled as Calico, and each one can be very different in colour and/or pattern. It appears that many of these strains are incompatible with each other.

An adult Calico retic showing typical patches of calico pattern. Picture credit: Anne and Thierry

It was assumed that Calico was a simple recessive gene, but breeding Calico to Calico (or het Calico) has proved that it is more complex than this. As with Calico patterns in other animals Calico retics are not born as Calico, but rather they undergo the colour and pattern change around maturity. From early breeding of Calico retics, those that underwent the colour change showed minimal and subtle variations. Males are extremely unlikely to be Calico, with around a 10 percent chance of a spot of Calico pattern coming out on a male, although they can still produce Calico offspring, which has also been shown to be the case in cats.

Calico can produce other different and interesting looking retics through parings that involve the Calico gene alongside others – for example NERD have produced their 'Flame' retic – an unusual tiger from a Calico breeding.

Rainbow

Prehistoric Pets recently proved Rainbow to be a new recessive morph after purchasing a pair of possible heterozygous Rainbow retics after a number were imported into the US. Rainbow retics appear to have very broken pattern with little yellow or orange in their base colours.

Incomplete dominant morphs

Tiger

The Tiger morph originally came from a wild-caught male found in central Sumatra that Karl Herman bred to a female in 1992 proving that the unusual pattern of the sire was genetic. Since half of the offspring showed the pattern of the father and half showed the normal pattern of the mother it was also demonstrated to be a dominant or incomplete dominant gene. The Tiger gene was later showed to be incomplete dominant in that there is a super form of it. The original male was reported to be around 3.7m (12ft) in length, but he was bred to several very large females, which has led to the slight misconception that the Tiger gene makes for large retics – it is not the Tiger gene, but the early breedings that lead to large Tigers.

The Tiger pattern is generally more elongated or even fully striped compared to the natural pattern, without the reticulated black patterning and reduced black lines. The rosettes along the side of the snake vary from white to yellow and are elongated and surrounded by black lines or speckling.

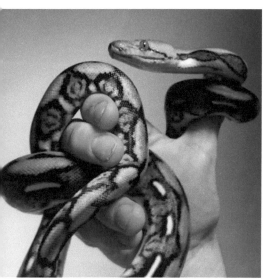

▲ *A hatchling Tiger retic. Picture credit: Rick Toeman*

▶ *Adult Tiger retic. Picture Credit: Jason Bert*

▲ *A Golden Child retic showing rich brown colouration and heavy black speckling. Picture credit: Mystic Genetics*

▲ *A Golden Child retic. Picture credit: Justin and Tina Monroe*

Golden Child (GC)

New England Reptile Distributors (NERD) have been credited with producing the first Golden Child (GC) babies after purchasing a wild-caught male. The original male was less than 2.4m (8ft) in length and thought to be from the Selayar Islands in Indonesia. The first clutch proved that GC was either a dominant or incomplete dominant gene in 2003–04.

The name GC was given to the morph by NERD not because of the colour of the snake, but because it was their 'golden child' project. Early GC retics were kept almost exclusively by NERD with very limited numbers of snakes being released to other breeders or keepers.

The appearance of GC retics varies greatly between snakes. The silver colour of the sides are not present and the white rosettes are reduced or gone. The black reticulations are also gone or reduced to speckling. The base colour of brown or orange often dominates the snake, and while some GC are light brown others are dark brown almost to the point of appearing black.

GC remains one of the most popular retic morphs available, and is widely available either on its own or in combination with other morphs, for example Albino or Motley.

▲ *A young Motley retic. Picture credit: Anne and Thierry*

Motley

The Motley gene occurred spontaneously in Bob Clark's collection from a female that he had produced from the first breeding of the original Clark albino retic. The first Motley was also an albino, and it wasn't until the original male was bred that a non-albino colour motley was produced.

The Motley is characterised by reduced side pattern and the dorsal pattern may appear as parallel lines all the way down the snake or almost perfect circles, or somewhere in between.

There is a super form of the Motley gene but early Super Motleys were said to be weak unless in combination with other genes such as albino. However, since then Super Motleys seem to have lost their reputation for being weak. They can vary from a very pale grey/white colour to a much darker silver/grey with very little in the way of pattern.

Platinum (Fire)

Platinum is the Incomplete Dominant gene for Ultra Ivory or Leucistic. Platinums were first bred by NERD in 2005.

The Platinum gene causes an overall lightening of colour in retics with higher amounts of yellow. Platinums can have slightly changed patterns with thinner or broken black markings on the back. The yellow in Platinum retics gets more intense as the animal grows into adulthood. The Platinum gene is very popular either as a single gene or in combination with others, producing beautiful bright retics with clean patterns.

It is generally recognised that there are two different strains of Platinum. For one strain the homozygous form is referred to as Ultra Ivory and for the other the homozygous form is referred to as Leucistic. The two strains behave similarly to those of Clark albino in that a reitc can be het for both Ultra Ivory and Leucistic. This produces a compound het referred to as Ivory, which is the equivalent to how Lavender is the compound het for White and Purple Clark albino. Both strains of Platinum are very similar in appearance and cannot reliably be distinguished by eye.

The homozygous form – Ultra Ivory – is the most colourful and highly patterned of the two strains. They tend to carry thin black lateral stripes and are marked with lemon yellows, oranges and silvers.

The homozygous form – Leucistic – generally produces pure white snakes with no colour or pattern and jet black eyes, although some can show traces of yellow.

The compound heterozygous form – referred to as Ivory – start life as pastel, off-white hatchlings with black eyes. They brighten with age to become almost white, often with sprinkles of black across the back and sides.

The first Ivory, Ultra Ivory and Leucistic retics in Europe were produced by James Coppen at Imperial Retics.

Lemonglow

There are different opinions about the Lemonglow morph. What is generally agreed is that the Lemonglow morph produces retics that are similar in appearance to Platinum retics. The first Lemonglow in the UK was imported by Peter Foulsham. Unlike Platinum retics, Lemonglow retics are all het for Leucistic and cannot be het for Ultra Ivory.

▶ *Platinum retic showing the increased yellow colour. Picture credit: Zack Thompson of Silver Spur Pythons*

Some people consider it likely that Lemonglow is another line of Platinum. Given the number of retics exported from Southeast Asia that have a Platinum-like appearance there could be many more lines of Platinum that are all similar in appearance and difficult to differentiate visually.

Note on Leucistic retics:

To date, evidence suggests that Leucistic retics have a much higher than average tendency to encounter health issues at a young age. Most notably a significant proportion of offspring develop fatal gastrointestinal issues. Despite this, several healthy adult specimens do exist in collections worldwide and have been able to reproduce. In 2015 Robert Euvino became the first in the United States, and possibly the world, to successfully breed and produce viable offspring from a Leucistic retic, a five-year-old female named Winter. His observations from this breeding were documented in 2016. In this document he recommends that anyone contemplating purchasing a Leucistic retic should "wait until the animal has attained significant size!" of at least 150–180cm (5–6ft) to be confident that the animal has not developed gastrointestinal problems.

Opinions differ, and evidence is unclear regarding whether Leucistic retics from Lemonglow lines have a lower chance of developing gastrointestinal problems than Leucistic retics from Platinum lines.

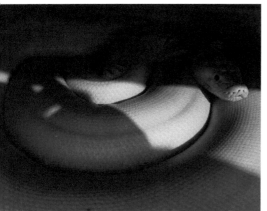

▲ *Adult Ivory retic. Picture credit: Zack Thompson of Silver Spur Pythons*

▶ *Hatchling Ultra Ivory retic. Picture credit: Matthew Genser*

▲ *An adult Lemon Glow retic. Picture credit: Darren Elson*

▶ *A Leuscistic retic, thought to be from a Lemonglow line. Picture credit: Robert Euvino*

Sunfire

Sunfire was thought to be first produced by Bob Clark in 2004. The original wild-caught Sunfire retic was actually shown to be a Super Sunfire, which was demonstrated when all the hatchlings in the first clutch were Sunfire. It is thought to be the only Incomplete Dominant gene that was caught from the wild in its homozygous form.

   The Sunfire gene mostly affects the colour of a retic by making the oranges and browns brighter and richer. Sunfire retics also often show a cleaner pattern than non-Sunfires – there is often less black speckling along the sides and back, and the reticulations sometimes form a stripe. The most telling feature of a Sunfire pattern compared to a wild

◀ ▼ *A beautiful Sunfire retic in natural sunlight and showing rich, bright orange colour. Picture credit: Darren Elson*

type is that the black on the tail fades rather than stops. The homozygous form of Sunfire – Super Sunfire – brightens colours even further.

There are several lines of Sunfire including Indo Sunfire, so named because it originated in Indonesia. In 2011 two males and one female Indo Sunfire retic were imported to Imperial Retics in the UK from a private breeding facility in Indonesia.

Jaguar

It is still unclear whether Jaguar is a Dominant or Incomplete Dominant gene, since it is not known if a homozygous form exists.

The Jaguar gene produces retics with a very clean pattern and little black speckling – the back is often striped and the colour is often light brown. The sides can vary from white rosettes, similar to the wild-type pattern, to much more elongated or joined-up white patches similar to a Tiger retic, while in most cases being lighter in colour than the normal colouring.

The Jaguar gene appears to be susceptible to neurological issues that are expressed by a head wobble or the inability to fully control the movement of the head and neck. It is possible that when combined with other genes this will be reduced, but that is currently not known.

▲ *Hatchling Jaguar Tiger retic. Picture credit: Zack Thompson of Silver Spur Pythons*

◄ *Beautiful young Jaguar retic. Picture credit: Kenny Lemmens*

▲ *Adult Phantom. Picture credit: Scott Cochrane of SC Pythons*

Phantom

Phantom was first produced by NERD. It is similar in appearance to the Orange Ghost Stripe retics although with more broken patterning along the back and darker colours along the sides. Phantom retics tend to show similar base colours to some of the brighter Golden Child retics. The homozygous form of Phantom is Blue Eyed Leucistic, very similar to the Leucustic gene produced by the Platinum gene, except for the eye colour. Phantom is compatible with OGS to produce retics which are referred to as the Cow morph.

Marble

The roots of the Marble gene are not fully known, but early Marbles were produced by Travis Kubes in Norfolk, Nebraska, in 2014. It is thought that the original marble was bred to a SD retic and a retic of Selayar locality, which can almost be thought of as two separate lines.

Marble retics show complex and tight or broken black patterning along the back. They often have high levels of browns and oranges and less grey and silver compared to the wild-type colours.

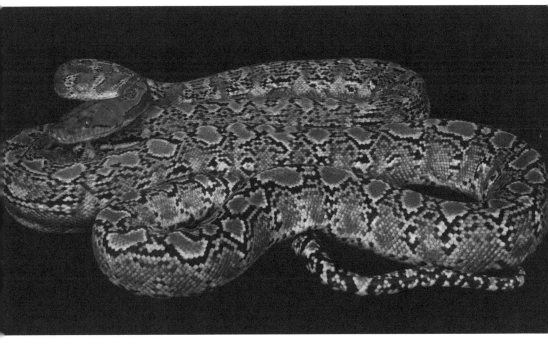

▲ *The broken black patterning on a marble retic. Picture credit: Mark Foster*

As mentioned earlier, the genetics and morphs of retics are complex and new morphs and combinations of morphs are being bred all the time. There is a wealth of information online and numerous groups where keepers can share their knowledge and new developments for those who want to learn more.

CHAPTER 6

LOCALITIES

Picture credit: John Wadsley

What is meant by localities?

In the wild, retics inhabit a wide area across Southeast Asia from mainland Thailand and surrounding countries to the island of Timor. Retics that are located in different areas, especially on isolated islands, have evolved characteristics including size, colour and pattern that are specific to that region and often differ between locations. These differing characteristics have led to retics being referred to by their locality. In particular, the two sub-species that were identified by Auliya et al were from specific island populations – Selayar Island and Jampea Island. It is possible that more localities will be recognised as sub-species in the future.

It should be noted that the descriptions of localities in this chapter are based on those that are generally used for captive populations. These descriptions do not necessary represent the majority of wild retics from each location. This is because there are a limited number of retic exporters in Southeast Asia – in recent years all exports have been from Indonesia – and keepers in Europe and the US are most interested in retics that have an unusual or unique appearance. This has led to captive retics that may differ in appearance to the typical appearance of the population in the wild.

To provide a comprehensive guide to retic populations and localities in the wild is beyond the scope of this book. This book focuses on the widely used descriptions for localities in captivity in Europe and the US.

Retic sizes can differ between localities with retics from mainland areas and large islands often being bigger than localities from smaller ones. These size differences have led to the terms Mainland, Dwarf and Super Dwarf, which keepers often abbreviate to ML, D and SD respectively. These terms are used in an attempt to classify the size or expected size that the retic will grow to. These terms can be misleading in some respects, since

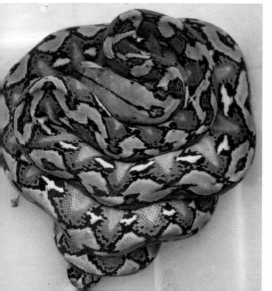

◄ *Beautiful pattern on this retic caught on Muna Island, southeast of Sulawesi. Picture credit: Jusuf Van Der Molen*

Dwarf retics are anything but small snakes so if you are considering a smaller one you still need to ensure you can provide suitable care for a reasonably large snake.

These terms are also used when the exact locality of a snake is unknown or if it has been bred with other localities in captivity. There is no categorical list for which localities fall into Mainland, Dwarf or Super Dwarf, and individual snakes can grow to different sizes that may fall outside of their expected size range.

This chapter lists some of the most common localities of retic that are available to keepers in the Europe and the US. It also links these localities with the size classifications of Mainland, Dwarf or Super Dwarf based on the expected size of retics from each locality. However, since there is no definitive classification some keepers may classify localities differently.

Mainland – the term Mainland is used to describe the group of localities that contain the very largest retics. Mainland retics are found on the continental portion of Southeast Asia including Myanmar, Laos, Thailand, Vietnam, Cambodia and Malaysia. The term is generally extended to include Sumatra, Java and to a lesser extent Bali since these areas are almost continuations of the continent and retic genetics here are similar to mainland populations. It is likely that their large size is due to the availability of large prey items, such as deer and wild pig. Some of the most commonly available mainland localities are Sumatra and Java. Retics described as mainland localities should be expected to attain very large size, up to and occasionally over 6.1m (20ft) in length. The term Mainland is sometimes used to refer to other large retics that are not considered as Dwarf or Super Dwarf, for example Sulawesi retics, however these localities are not strictly Mainland localities.

Dwarf and Super Dwarf Retics – the term Dwarf retic can be misleading since a Dwarf can reach large sizes and it is difficult to say exactly what counts as a Dwarf locality. However, the label Dwarf is often applied to medium-sized retic localities where sizes tend to range from 2.4–4.6m (8–15ft). These often come from islands where the retic population is geographically isolated from mainland areas and the population has evolved separately from other retics. Being isolated on islands, it is thought that reduced availability and a smaller size of prey has led to Dwarf and Super Dwarf localities reaching generally smaller sizes than Mainland localities. Some examples of localities that are commonly agreed to be Dwarf retics include Jampea and Selayar.

It was originally thought that the term Super Dwarf was created as a marketing strategy to sell retics to those who were not willing to keep a giant snake. Some people still claim that there are no localities that are truly Super Dwarf. However, it is now commonly accepted that some of the very smallest retic localities should be referred to as Super

Dwarf. These often grow to 1.8–3.0m (6–10ft) and include Kayuadi, Kalaotoa and Madu.

The growth rates of Super Dwarf retics was investigated by hobbyist keeper David Bellis in 2005. He compared the growth rate of four reticulated pythons – three were considered Super Dwarf and one was a Mainland. Over a six-month period he varied the frequency of the feeding between the animals while keeping the relative size of the meals approximately the same. There was a direct effect on growth rate on the Super Dwarf retics – the more frequently they were fed, the faster they grew. However, even the Super Dwarf with the most frequent feeding was not able to match the size and growth of the Mainland retic that was fed less frequently. This small-scale experiment shows that while diet plays a factor in the growth of retics it seems genetics are a stronger influence and that in the study there were differences in growth between the Super Dwarfs and Mainland retics.

For Super Dwarf retics that have been bred with Mainland retics it is common for breeders to track the percentage of Super Dwarf line that is in the snake. For example, consider a pure Super Dwarf locality as being 100 percent Super Dwarf being bred with a Mainland locality (considered as 0 percent Super Dwarf) – the offspring would be classed as 50 percent Super Dwarf. If a 50 percent Super Dwarf was bred to a 100 percent Super Dwarf, the percentage of Super Dwarf of the offspring would be 75 percent (50+100)/2).

For retics that have been bred from a Super Dwarf and a Mainland, the percentage refers to what proportion of the line is Super Dwarf. These percentages of Super Dwarf do not mean that the snakes will grow to that percentage of the length of a Mainland, or even the percentage difference between a Mainland and Super Dwarf. The influence of Super Dwarf and Mainland can vary between retics, since the offspring will have genes from a larger and a smaller parent. In general the offspring will reach a size somewhere between the two, but some may grow as large as a Mainland and some may stay closer to the size of a Super Dwarf.

"Recessive morph into Super Dwarf retics equals a life's work." Credit: UK Exotics.

- 0% SD (ML albino) x 100% SD = 50% SD (het albino)

- 50% SD (het albino) x 50% SD (het albino) = 50% SD (albino)

- 50% SD (albino) x 100% SD = 75% SD (het albino)

- 75% SD (het albino) x 75% SD (het albino) = 75% SD (albino)

- 75% SD (albino) x 100% SD = 87.5% SD (het albino)

- 87.5% SD (het albino) x 87.5% SD (het albino) = 87.5% SD (albino)

The above process is around 25 years' worth of selectively breeding recessive morphs into Super Dwarf lines.

There are relatively few genetic morphs that are thought to have originated in Dwarf and Super Dwarf retics – Anery is the only morph thought to have originated in Super Dwarf retics. As such, the majority of morphs that are labelled as Super Dwarf retics have been bred into Super Dwarf lines from larger retics and will often be sold with the percentage of Super Dwarf stated.

In general, Super Dwarf retics of a specific morph will cost more than non-Super Dwarf example of the same morph, especially for recessive genes. This is because of the time that it takes to breed a genetic morph into a Super Dwarf line. UK Exotics presents this process well (see below) using albino as an example and say that "Recessive morph into Super Dwarf retics equals a life's work."

Common localities

Mainland (ML) – up to and over 6.1m (20ft)

Borneo – up to 6.1m (20ft)
Java – up to 6.1m (20ft)
Sumatra – up to and over 6.1m (20ft)
Sulawesi including Makassar and Bantaeng – up to and over 6.1m (20ft)
Thailand – up to 6.1m (20ft)
Bali – up to 6.1m (20ft)

Borneo

This is a very large island in the Malay Archipelago. A very limited number of retics from Borneo have been imported to Europe and the US in the last 15 years. The small numbers that have been imported had fairly regular patterns and large dorsal patches. Retics from Borneo can grow up to 6.1m (20ft) in length.

◄ *A Borneo locality retic. Picture credit: Rodney Boalich*

Java

This is an island in Indonesia with Sumatra to the west, Bali to the east and Borneo to the north. There is a lot of variation in the pattern of retics from Java, although they are often regular and similar to those found in Borneo. Given that Java is surrounded by other retic habitats, it may be that the population of snakes has remained less isolated than other localities, which may explain the variation between retics from Java and the similarity that some share with other localities. Retics from Java can grow up to 6.1m (20ft) in length.

▶ *A young Java locality retic. Picture credit: Larion Polacsek*

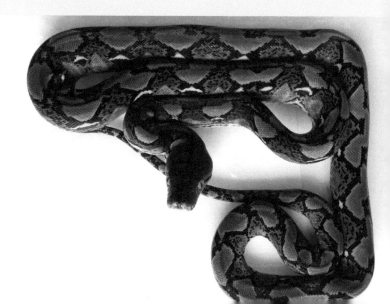

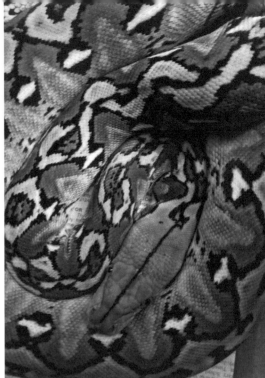

▲ *A Sulawesi retic showing complex black patterning on the neck, which gradually becomes triangular further down the body. Picture credit: Justin and Tina Monroe*

Sulawesi (Makassar, Bantaeng)

This is a large island east of Borneo. Bantaeng is a regency of South Sulawesi, while Makassar is the provincial capital of South Sulawesi. It is possible that retics labelled as Makassar or Bantaeng may be the same as Sulawesi and that the label refers to where they were caught, or they may be separate lines of Sulawesi retics. However, the majority of keepers will not know the exact location of the retic's origin because the labels for a snake's locality are often given from where the snake was shipped rather than where it was caught, which makes it difficult to assess whether Makassar and Banaeng retics are separate lines.

Retics from Sulawesi have generally regular, sometimes very triangular dorsal patterns. They have yellow to brown heads with grey and silver flanks. They are considered to be some of the biggest retics, growing up to and over 6.1m (20ft) in length.

Sumatra

This is a large island west of Java and south of Malaysia in the Indian Ocean. The appearance of retics from Sumatra can vary considerably from tight reticulations to a more joined-up, stripe-like pattern. It is thought that many of the earliest wild-caught retics that were brought

▲ An adult Sumatran retic showing attractive silver sides and regular triangular reticulations. Picture credit: Justin and Tina Monroe

into captivity in the UK and US were from Sumatra. Retics from here are some of the largest and can reach over 6.1m (20ft) in length.

Thailand

Thailand is a country on the mainland Southeast Asia, bordering Cambodia, Myanmar, Laos and Malaysia. Most Thai retics are similar in appearance to retics in Malaysia. While Thai retics are rare in Europe and the US some Thai retics have been selectively exported because of their yellow heads. Retics from Thailand and surrounding countries on the mainland generally grow to similar lengths and all are capable of reaching large sizes.

◄ An adult Thai locality retic showing beautiful iridescence. Picture credit: Christian Kirchner

Bali

Bali is an Indonesian Island between Java to the west and Lombok to the east. Bali could be thought of as an extension of the mainland along with Sumatra and Java since wild retics on Bali typically grow large and exhibit colours and patterns similar to other mainland localities. Bali retics that showed yellow heads have been selectively exported to Europe and the US, although only a fraction of retics on Bali have yellow heads.

Bali retics can grow large and in this respect they should be considered as a Mainland locality. Bali retics generally grow to around 4.3–5.5m (14–18ft) but females especially are capable of growing up to 6.1m (20ft). In captivity Bali retics are sometimes described as a Dwarf locality that will grow to around 3.6–4.3m (12–14ft) in length; be aware that if you get a Bali retic it could get considerably bigger than this.

▼ *A Bali locality retic. Picture credit: Weston Wenner*

Dwarf/Medium sized – 2.4–4.5m (8–15ft)

Jampea – 3.0–3.7m (10–12ft), max 4.9m (16ft)
Selayar – 3.0–4.6m (10–15ft), max 5.2m (17ft)
Ambon – 3.6–4.3m (12–14ft), max 4.9m (16ft)

Note: The maximum sizes given for Dwarf and Super Dwarf localities are a sensible upper limit for size rather than an absolute maximum.

AMBON

SELAYAR

JAMPEA

Jampea (Jamp)

As of 2002, reticulated pythons from Jampea have been classified as a separate subspecies of reticulated python, as detailed in the paper by Auliya Et al published in 2002. Tunah Jampea is the second largest of the Selayar Islands, which lie off the coast of South Sulawesi. Jampea retics commonly have less black patterning, often with high greys/silvers and less rich oranges and golds in the base colour. They generally grow to around 3.0–3.7m (10–12ft) in length.

◀ *Jampea locality retic. Picture credit: Joanna Aldwinckle*

Selayar

As of 2002, reticulated pythons from the Island of Selayar have also been classified as a separate sub-species. The Selayar Islands lie off the coast of South Sulawesi and form a small archipelago and the island of Selayar is the largest of these islands. Retics from here often have broken pattern or joined-up diamond patterns along the back and smaller areas of silver along the sides. Retics from Selayar generally grow to around 3.0–4.6m (10–15ft) in length.

► *A Selayar locality retic. Picture credit: Darren Elson*

Ambon

This is a small island south of Seram and east of Sulawesi and it is part of Maluku Islands. Ambon locality retics can look similar to Java and Bali retics and occasionally have yellow heads, but this is probably the minority since retics from Ambon can have very variable colour and pattern. Ambon retics generally grow to 3.6–4.3m (12–14ft), but have been reported to grow up to 5.5m (18ft) in length. Ambon retics are one of the larger Dwarf localities.

► *A wild caught female Ambon locality retic. Picture credit: John Wadsley*

Super Dwarf – 1.8–3.0m (6–10ft)

Kalaotoa – 1.8–2.1m (6–7ft), max 2.7m (9ft)
Madu – 1.8–2.4m (6–8ft), max 3.0m (10ft)
Kayuadi – 2.1–2.7m (7–9ft), max 3.0m (10ft)

Note: *The maximum sizes given for Dwarf and Super Dwarf localities are a sensible upper limit rather than an absolute maximum.*

KAYUADI

KALAOTOA

MADU

Kalaotoa

This is an island in the Flores Sea, southeast of Selayar and Jampea. Retics from Kalaotoa often have little yellow or orange colour, with more greys, browns and blacks. The dorsal pattern can be tight and detached. Kalaotoa retics grow to around 1.5–2.4m (5–8ft) in length.

▶ *A Kalaotoa locality retic. Picture credit: Eric Lee*

▲ *A Madu island locality retic. Picture credit: Scott Hood*

▲ *Kayuadi mother on a clutch of eggs. Picture credit: Heather Hodsdon and Dean Turner, The Reptile Room*

Madu

Pulau Madu is a very small island just south of Kalaotoa. Madu retics are similar in appearance to Kalaotoa examples, but retain some of the yellow and gold base colours that are common in many Mainland localities. Madu retics grow to around 1.8–3.0m (6–10ft) in length.

Kayuadi

This is one of the small Selayar Islands. Kayuadi retics are similar in appearance to Kalaotoa and Madu examples. Some people claim that retics from Kayuadi should be considered Dwarf rather than Super Dwarf. Kayuadi retics grow to around 1.8–3.0m (6–10ft) in length.

Other locality retics

The following list shows less common localities that might be used to describe the type of retics, although again it is not possible to provide a list of all possible locations.

● Buton
● Flores
● Karompa
● Malaysia
● Maluku Islands
● Myanmar

● Sunda Islands
● Talaud Islands
● Timor Island
● Vietnam

● Philippines – Very few retics have been exported from the Philippines, but since there are over 7000 islands in the Philippines it is likely that there is a huge variation in retics.

▶ *Snakes from Karompa are also considered as Super Dwarf retics. The island of Karompa is within Southern Sulawesi and close to Kalaotoa and Madu. Picture credit: Roxanne Liz Ronne.*

COMMON ISSUES AND HEALTH PROBLEMS

Picture credit: Scott Cochrane

Common health issues

This book does not provide medical advice. If you are in any doubt about the health of your retic you should take it to a specialist reptile vet as soon as possible.

As mentioned in the beginning of this book, if you are considering keeping a retic it is recommended that you locate and research the vets in your area who specialise in reptiles. In particular, you will want to talk to a veterinary practice to ensure they would be willing to treat a retic should the need arise – not all vets will be willing to deal with a large retic in distress, even if they do have some experience of dealing with smaller, more common exotic species.

If you have a large number of reptiles or snakes already it is good practice to quarantine new animals. This will help to prevent the spread of disease or parasites until you are confident that the new animal is healthy.

The conditions covered below are not exhaustive but do highlight some of the more common issues related to retics in captivity and for many snake species. Most health issues can be avoided by providing good set-ups and suitable care.

Snake Mites

These are a relatively common problem for reptile keepers – even with good standards of cleanliness they can sometimes be transferred to your animals. Snake mites (Ophionyssus natricis) are a parasite that can affect snakes and many lizard species. These mites feed on the blood of the snake and can carry disease. They are around 1mm (0.04in) in length and black or dark brown in colour. They are able to travel from one host to another and can walk across rooms or between enclosures. While a few mites do not pose a big risk to a healthy retic, if the number of mites increases they can become a problem and cause anaemia in the snake, so it is best to treat them as soon as they are spotted.

The most common way for mites to get to your retics is from other reptile collections, reptile shops or in substrate and equipment that has been produced or stored in reptile-inhabited places. Mites and other parasites can also be brought into a collection from wild-caught animals, although the majority of retics in the UK are captive bred.

If your retic spends a lot of time submerged in water this could be a sign that it has mites, as it tries to reduce the irritation and drown them. However, this could also be a sign that the snake is preparing to shed its skin or that the enclosure is too hot, while some retics just seem to enjoy spending time in water. If you suspect mites, check in the water bowl for small black specks. If these can be squashed with your fingernails and leave a red smear then the snake probably has mites.

Mites can be difficult to eliminate – they are small and often not noticed until they have established and bred. Their life cycle is around four weeks (dependent on conditions including temperature) and adults will lay eggs on the snake or in the substrate. Treatment often kills the adults but leaves the eggs to hatch. They can also live for several days away from the snake and can travel between enclosures and rooms looking for a host.

There are different approaches to treating mites – the two most common are using insecticide sprays or predatory mites, which are released into the enclosure and will feed on snake mites. If you need help to determine which method to use, consult a vet and always follow the directions for whichever method you decide on.

When a snake has mites it is best to treat it and its enclosure as soon as possible with whichever treatment you prefer, and ensure the area surrounding the enclosure is kept clean to prevent the problem escalating. If you have multiple snakes in the same room you may wish to consider treating all of your animals and their enclosures. Avoid handling the snake as much as possible while treating the mites as this will help to prevent them from spreading.

Respiratory Infection (RI)

Respiratory infections can be a problem for retics and other tropical and sub-tropical snake species. These infections are linked to incorrect humidity levels – either too high or too low – which then makes the snake susceptible to lung infection. An RI can sometimes be identified by the snake's breathing sounding like a whistle, a gurgle or as a prolonged huff. In advanced cases it may be possible to see mucus or bubbles around the nostrils or mouth. An RI usually needs to be treated by a vet and will probably require a course of antibiotics, so if you suspect your retic of having an RI get your snake to a vet as soon as possible.

Burns

These can be a common injury in snakes if the heat source is not set up correctly, due to it coming into contact or being too close to its heat source. This is why it is crucial to have a suitable heat source that is fully guarded and on a thermostat. Heat mats can also cause burns in large-bodied snakes, which is why heat mats are generally not recommended for retics.

Should the worst happen and your retic burns itself on the heat source it should to be treated by a vet. The wound will need to be kept clean and you may wish to consider changing substrate to kitchen towel while it heals. Once it has healed the snake may struggle to shed around the wound, but for minor burns this should only be for a few sheds and the wound will not leave any scar tissue. More serious burns could scar and the snake may have issues with shedding throughout its life as a result.

Obesity/overweight

Large pythons have very efficient metabolisms and can go for long periods of time without food. For such a snake, being obese puts a large strain on the internal organs around which fat is stored. For a healthy retic, monitor the body condition of the snake and adjust the feeding accordingly to prevent it from becoming obese. For an obese retic, reduce the size and frequency of meals, and handle the snake more regularly so that the snake gets more exercise to help retain muscle condition.

Other wounds

These should be treated a bit like burns. The snake should be taken to a vet and the injury should be kept clean to allow it time to heal.

Inclusion Body Disease (IBD)/arena virus

This is most commonly found in boa constrictors – boas can carry the arena virus for long periods of time and it is often carried without harm to the snake. However, the arena virus can develop into IBD, which is a virus that affects the nervous system. It is not clear whether pythons can carry the arena virus without developing IBD. While it is very rare in pythons there have been cases of pythons with IBD. The symptoms of IBD in boas may include refusing food and regurgitating meals, leading to weight loss. They may also develop problems with the respiratory system, which may look like an RI. IBD will generally progress towards problems with the nervous system, including head tremors and loss of motor function. It is worth being aware of the symptoms and if IBD is suspected your retic should be taken to the vet immediately for a formal diagnosis and possible treatment.

Prevention is better than cure for all of the conditions covered in this chapter. With good maintenance and care these issues can be avoided in most cases.

Glossary

Bioactive In reference to a reptile set-up, this is the use of natural methods to self-clean an enclosure, which includes bacteria and invertebrates that feed upon waste material.

CITES Convention of International Trade in Endangered Species of Wild Fauna and Flora.

Class A taxonomic rank used to categorise wildlife.

Cloaca The posterior orifice on the underside of the snake before the tail.

Co-dominant gene Where a combination of a recessive and a dominant genetic trait appear together to produce combination that differs from either trait individually.

Cold-blooded *see* Endothermic.

Dominant gene A genetic trait is dominant if the gene can be expressed when it is passed from only one parent to the offspring.

Dwarf A term used to describe retics that are expected to reach mid-size based on their locality or the locality of their ancestors.

Enclosure The area used to house a snake.

Endothermic (cold-blooded) Animals that require environmental temperatures to moderate their body temperature.

Family A taxonomic rank used to categorise wildlife.

Genus A taxonomic rank used to categorise wildlife.

Hatchling A retic in its first year of life.

Heat guard A frame used to prevent the snake from coming into direct contact with a heat source.

Heat Lamps and bulbs A bulb that is used to generate heat in an enclosure – these can be light emitting or non-light emitting (usually ceramic).

Heterozygous Where a snake carries only a single copy of a gene for a specific genetic trait.

Hides A piece of decoration used to provide a space for the snake to hide in.

Homozygous Where a snake carries two copies of the gene for a specific genetic trait – one from each parent.

Humidity The amount of moisture or water vapour within a specific environment.

Hygrometer A device used to measure humidity.

Impaction A condition where ingested items, e.g. substrate, and faeces become compressed and can become stuck in the intestine.

In blue The state when a snake prepares to shed its skin.

Inclusion Body Disease (IBD)/arena virus A disease that can affect boas and pythons.

Incomplete-Dominant gene Where the heterozygous form of a genetic trait is visually different from retics that do not carry the gene, and the homozygous form is different to the heterozygous form.

Juvenile A retic aged between 18 months and sexual maturity, generally between two and four years of age.

Line-bred Breeding for specific characteristics or genetics from closely related animals.

Localities A term used to describe retics that originate from different geographic areas.

Mainland A term used to describe retics that are expected to reach large sizes based on their locality or the locality of their ancestors.

Moist hide A hide that is filled with damp substrate to increase humidity in an isolated area.

Monsoon A seasonal effect of the prevailing wind which affects rainfall and temperatures.

Morph A term used to describe a genetic trait that affects the appearance of a snake.

Order and suborder Taxonomic ranks used to categorise wildlife.

Racking system A system of drawers or racks that can fit a number of plastic tubs to house snakes.

Recessive gene A genetic trait where the snake needs to inherit two copies of the gene for the trait to be expressed.

Reptile radiator/heat plates A type of heating used for reptile enclosures, often low in profile and covering a wider area than a bulb.

Respiratory infection An infection of the respiratory tract.

Shedding The act of a snake sloughing the top layer of its skin.

Snake mites Parasites that feed on the blood of snakes and some lizards

Species A taxonomic rank used to categorise wildlife.

Spot clean To clean only the soiled part of an enclosure.

Subspecies A taxonomic rank used to categorise wildlife.

Substrate The material used to line the bottom of the enclosure.

Super Dwarf A term used to describe retics that are expected to reach small sizes based on their locality or the locality of their ancestor.

Tap training A conditioning technique used when handling snakes, where the snake is stroked before being handled.

Temperature gradient The transition in temperatures between the hot and cool side of the enclosure.

Thermal blocking Uneven distribution of heat through the snake by contact with heat sources that raise surface temperatures.

Thermoregulation The act of a snake controlling its body temperature by using environmental conditions.

Thermostat (stat) Device used to control the temperatures in an enclosure.

Tube heater A heat source that can be used in large enclosures.

Ultraviolet light A frequency of light that is used for vitamin D synthesis in animals.

Ventilation The provision of fresh air in an enclosure.

Vivarium An enclosure that is secure on all sides except the front, which is usually clear glass or plastic that opens along runners or on hinges.

Wild caught An animal that has been brought into captivity from the wild.

Wild type The natural colour and pattern of a snake.

Yearling A retic aged between the age of 12 and 18 months.

References

Predation on sun bears by reticulated python in East Kalimantan, Indonesian Borneo. Fredriksson, 2005. dare.uva.nl/document/2/39161

Tales of Giant Sankes, 1997. www.academia.edu/964415/1997_Tales_of_Giant_Snakes

Review of the reticulated python with the description of new subspecies from Indonesia, Auiya et al, 2002. www.researchgate.net/publication/11246968_Review_of_the_reticulated_python_Python_reticulatus_Schneider_1801_with_the_description_of_new_subspecies_from_Indonesia

Wikipedia. en.wikipedia.org/wiki/Pythonidae

Reticulated pythons in Sumatra: biology, harvesting and sustainability. Shine et al, 1999. reticulatedpython.info/me/papers/226reticulatedpythons.pdf

The reptile database: Malaopython reticulatus. reptile-database.reptarium.cz/species?genus=Malayopython&species=reticulatus

Reptile Forums UK. www.reptileforums.co.uk/forums/

Alex and Susi, UK Exotics; Dwarf and Super Dwarf retics – presentation. www.ukexotics.com/retic-presentation.html

Instructables; Reptile tank heating and lighting guide. www.instructables.com/id/Reptile-tank-heating-and-lighting-guide/?ALLSTEPS

David Bellis in 2005.reticulatedpython.info/misc2.html

Serpent Exotics; Reticulated pythons. www.serpentexotics.com/reticulated_python_wiki.html

Jungle giants: Assessing sustainable harvesting in a difficult-to-survey species. Natusch et al, 2016. www.ncbi.nlm.nih.gov/pmc/articles/PMC4938584/

Sustainable management of the trade in reticulated python skins in Indonesia and Malaysia, Natusch et al, 2016. www.iucn.org/sites/dev/files/content/documents/2016/natusch_et_al_2016_sustainable_management_of_the_trade_in_reticulated_python_skins.pdf

Shine et al, 1999. Study of reptile slaughterhouse. onlinelibrary.wiley.com/doi/10.1046/j.1365-2435.1998.00179.x/pdf

Meet the Agta, a tribe where a quarter of men have been attacked by giant snakes. phenomena.nationalgeographic.com/2011/12/12/meet-the-agta-a-tribe-where-a-quarter-of-men-have-been-attacked-by-giant-snakes/

Locality retics. localityretics.wordpress.com/

Convention of International Trade in Endangered Species of Wild Fauna and Flora. www.cites.org/eng/resources/quotas/index.php#

Constrictors.com archived content. web.archive.org/web/20080314052532/http://www.constrictors.com:80/Collection/ReticulatedPythons/PiebaldReticulatedPython.html

Gastrointestinal Disorders in Leucistic Reticulated Pythons: Theories and Observations, 2016. Robert L. Euvino. docs.google.com/document/d/1N58x59Y3HGlJQhyoy2lxbDesNT3oCLAR27jkRvCCUKA/edit#

Bob Clark website. www.bobclark.com/#&panel1-1

Facebook Groups:

The Retic Nation FB Group

Reticulated Pythons Worldwide

Retic-Eugenics

Acknowledgments

I'd like to thank everyone who has helped me through the process of writing this book, whether through proof-reading, answering questions or providing photos.

In particular I'd like to thank:
- My wife Natasha, who started my passion in retics when she bought Chaos
- My family and friends, who have read the manuscript, especially Nicole Lowe,
- Jayne Warren and Mary Grinsted.
- Ben Way for editing the text.
- Geoff Borin for cover and interior design.

All of the retic keepers who have shared their expertise, especially:
- Scott Cochrane of SC Pythons for your advice throughout.
- Tyree Jimerson and Travis Warren for your input with the chapter on genetics.
- Jakub Kyzl Reptile for your input with the Localities chapter.
- Charles Thompson of Snakes 'N' Adders for your input with the Localities chapter.
- Wolfgang Keil for your input with the Localities chapter.
- Steve Dawson for your input with giant retics and your advice throughout.
- Everyone who has provided photos.

CPSIA information can be obtained
at www.ICGtesting.com
Printed in the USA
BVHW021542020919
557353BV00009B/104/P